Successful Ministry
to the Retarded

by

Elmer L. Towns

and

Roberta L. Groff

Moody Press • Chicago

Library of Congress Card Catalog Number: 70-181589
ISBN: 0-8024-8425-5

Second Printing, 1974

Printed in the United States of America

CONTENTS

Introduction

"Why *me*, Lord?" The anguished cry springs involuntarily to the heart if not the lips of parents who discover for the first time that their child is mentally retarded. Some engage in soul-searching self-recrimination, seeking a cause within themselves, while others plunge to the depths of depression, certain that social stigma will ostracize them from former contacts. A few are able to quickly adjust to what they accept as part of the "all things [that] work together for good to them that love God."

At the very least, the first two courses may well compound the problem. Wrapped in their own cocoon of self-pity, the parents deprive the extra-needy child of the love without which all children fail to realize their potential.

"For weeks, I couldn't bear to look at my baby," admitted the mother of a Mongoloid daughter. "I turned away my head as quickly as I could prop her bottle on a pillow and leave her alone." She faced the problem without the indwelling strength of faith in God. When that mother's helplessness and need had been used by the Holy Spirit to lead her to Christ, God's love overflowed into the life of a baby which at birth had been declared by doctors as "untrainable." Acceptance by the parents led to acceptance by their church. Eight years later the little girl was reading, to the amazement of her doctors.

But even acceptance cannot presuppose knowledge of

how to spiritually reach and train a child with any of the varying degrees of mental retardation. Should a parent assume — as even some Christian psychologists have done — that such a child is beyond reach? Can it be taken for granted that the mentally retarded child will by his handicap be held unaccountable before God — regardless of his grasp of other knowledge?

Clear, documented, workable answers are presented in SUCCESSFUL MINISTRY TO THE RETARDED, which is based on the premise that *the church's ministry is twofold: first, a ministry to the retardate himself; and second, a ministry to the family.* Not infrequently the retardate's parents and siblings, led to acceptance and ability to cope with a family problem, have widened their outreach to include a personal ministry to other similar families.

A second thesis of this book is that *the church can structure a program for the mentally retarded involving teaching content, building healthy mental attitudes, and developing social and Christian skills.* Chapter 5 deals with this aspect of ministry.

Third is the thesis that *the church can have an active, organized ministry of evangelism, attempting to win the mentally retarded to Christ.* Chapter 4 contains this discussion. Since there are five million mentally retarded persons in America, since three hundred mentally retarded babies are born each day, and since 90 percent of all these are in the community rather than in institutions, the churches should be more concerned about winning them to Jesus Christ.

Implementing and augmenting these ministries must be *ample resources for the conduct of proper Christian education for mentally retarded, such as facilities, program, and personnel.* This aspect is covered in chapters 6 and 7.

Finally, because compassion is vital for success in such a ministry, *a church must provide a program of spiritual care for appropriate ministry at times of major crises — either through its own direct care or through referrals to other agencies.* See chapter 9.

Those motivated to active participation in such a ministry will find the bibliography and footnotes helpful for further research. Appendixes provide more technical treatment of the subject.

"As each star differs in brightness, so do the children of men. Yet each serves its purpose in 'One nation under God' and each is entitled to an opportunity to achieve his full potential — to grow physically, emotionally, intellectually, socially and spiritually."[1]

PART I

Foundation for Ministry

1

What Is Mental Retardation?

THE WORDS *mental retardation* carry a highly emotional charge within our culture, evoking confusion, misunderstanding, and fear. Parents often experience deep guilt and self-pity when retardation is evidenced in their child. While retardation repulses some people, it tugs at the hearts of others whose attitude says, "I want to help this child. Won't someone please show me how?"

Simply put, mental retardation is the result of injury to or disease of the brain either before or after birth.* These injuries or diseases either completely destroy the brain tissue or harm it in such a way that it can no longer develop and function properly. As a result, the brain-injured person cannot function as do normal human beings.

Since various diseases and injuries harm the brain in varying degrees of intensity, there are many differing states of mental retardation. In this broad classification fall mongolism, cerebral palsy, retarded emotional growth, and such physical complications as sight and hearing handicaps, slow and incomplete motor-ability development, and mild forms of epilepsy.

The retarded individuals are classified by professional instructors into two intellectual and educational categories according to their ability to learn: First is the *educable retarded* group, and second is the *trainable retarded* group.

* An expanded discussion of mental retardation is found in Appendix II, "Definition of Mental Retardation"

The *educable* mentally retarded child is mildly retarded, with an IQ range of approximately 55 to 75 or 80. Although mental development is slow, he can and does usually attend public school classes where he learns basic fundamental skills. He does not handle abstractions and concepts well, he is less able to generalize than the average student, his attention span is short, and he has poor concentrative abilities, but he is able, in a limited way, to find a place in society. Such a child can and does benefit in a regular Sunday school class.

The *trainable* retarded child, however, is more severely limited. With an IQ which ranges from 30 to 55, he will be unable to assimilate expected academic learning. Although he may be able to learn facts, those facts will be meaningless because he cannot transfer and relate them to new situations. However, he can probably learn those things which pertain to self-care, social habits, and to his adjustment in his immediate and familiar surroundings.

Sometimes these children will show retarded physical and emotional growth, and a distinct physical handicap may also be present. Although the educable child can go to school and eventually work to support himself, the trainable person is limited in terms of academic skills and will require closer supervision throughout his life-span. Nevertheless, God created him as a human being and intended that he should be given an equal measure of love.

The sociological implications of retardation label it as a "problem" in this technologically sophisticated society. However, in less complex societies, it is not looked upon as a disaster, for persons of limited mental ability are often capable of gaining superiority by virtue of other assets than those measured by intelligence tests. For example, they can make successful hunters, fishermen, or tribal dancers.[1]

In our society there are retardates who are farm hands, factory workers, mothers' helpers and similar manual laborers. Although they may perform a simple operational task, they have little educational and vocational ambition or ability. They are "subcultural" in our society but may not even be that in a different, less sophisticated society.

The trainable retardates will never of themselves fit into the average way of living, which is perhaps why there are factions which invariably try to connect retardation and delinquency. However, no such generalities can be drawn. Some law-enforcement authorities, who perhaps misunderstand retardation, tend to generalize that these people are destined for a life of delinquency. While some retardates do participate in social misconduct, Dr. Lawson Lowrey explains that the unacceptable behavior of the retarded is the working out of their conflicts over being different and inferior persons. "If the deficient juvenile keeps company with those leaning toward delinquency, he might go along with their misbehavior for two reasons: he wants to be accepted, and he doesn't think independently and well enough to judge their character. However, the mentally retarded respond to both good and bad influences."[2] Herein lies the real importance of the retardate's religious training and of his presence in a Sunday school class, for he needs to learn that God is good, and that God wants him to respond to the good things and to shun the bad.

Causes of Retardation

Retardates are born to average, brilliant and dull parents alike, and into both highly educated and illiterate families. All racial, social, religious, economic and national groups are affected.[3] Even so gifted a man as John F. Kennedy had a mentally retarded sister.

Medical science has progressed far enough to disprove Dr. C. B. Davenport's 1911 law that "inheritance of mental defect appears quite general, definite and easily predictable."[4] Science now agrees that this law has no basis in fact. Parents tend to be self-incriminating about retardation until they become convinced that their parentage is not responsible for this present child, and that they must not hold themselves responsible for retardation which appears in future generations *unless* they have diseases which can harm those children. They will only inhibit any happy, normal growth in their retarded child if they refuse to achieve an understanding and acceptance of mental deficiency.

One authority on retardation and inheritance explains that on those occasions when "mental deficiency *does* have a hereditary source, it *regularly appears in each succeeding generation.* Members of the genetically deficient family either go on to reproduce without any conscience about contributing more deficiency to society or they have no realization of deficiency."[5]

Retardation results when there is incomplete development or destruction of tissues of either the brain or the other parts of the central nervous system. The greatest percentage of retardation occurs in prenatal stages,[6] with environment, genetics and infection as the three main causes. Overexposure to X rays as well as certain illnesses and infections, and glandular disorders during pregnancy can harm the baby. Prolonged labor, hemorrhage or lack of oxygen may injure the child's brain. An attack of German measles in the mother may harm a fetus, as may the presence of the Rh blood factor in all but the first pregnancy, when the blood systems within mother and baby differ in such a way that the interplay harms or kills the unborn child. Those things causing retardation after birth are accident, poisoning, chemical imbalance and disease.[7]

Brain damage resulting in retardation evidently has many causes, some of which have not been completely defined or researched.

Mongolism, technically known as Downs Syndrome, makes up one-third of all retardation. The Mongoloid is born from a pregnancy during which genetic imbalance has occurred. This chemical "mistake" takes place when the sperm and ova meet, but the medical world has only speculated why this happens. "However, it is one of the results of women having repeated exposure to large amounts of X ray. Other harmful agents may include such viruses as hepatitis and such drugs as LSD."[8]

A woman's age can also affect the health of the ova which she produces. Since the ova in her body has been there since her birth, it thus has been affected by both the good and harmful factors of her health. When she becomes pregnant near or at age forty, her chances of producing a Mongoloid are greater than at age twenty simply because disease and infection have had twice as many years to play upon the entire body, including the ova.[9]

Doctors can recognize the Mongoloid child at birth, and his features remain distinctive through life. Take Judy, for example. Her condition was easily recognized by her rounded face, enlarged tongue, deep indentations at the corners of her eyes, yellowish skin, stumpy arms and short, broad neck. Formerly medical students were taught that all Mongoloids were profoundly retarded, but now it is known that they may have an IQ as high as 70.

Another third of all retardates have suffered *organic* brain damage, which occurred neither from disease nor faulty genetic influence, but because the brain received some kind of destructive physical injury or alteration.[10] Thus some parts, specifically those having to do with intelligence, no longer function normally. Brain tissue can be destroyed in the prenatal stages by prolonged labor, pelvic pressure, hemorrhage, or lack of oxygen. Any organic brain damage which occurs after birth can be due to poisoning, accidental blows to the head, or glandular disturbance.[11] All of these things can kill brain tissue, and to this date scientists have found no way to make it alive and functional again.

PHYSICAL COMPLICATIONS

Initially, retardation implies a loss in some degree of intellectual functioning, but physical problems also ensue because the brain is no longer functioning in its normal capacity. Whether the brain damage has been organic or genetic, the central nervous system is impaired. Sometimes this organic impairment includes the death of certain tissues of the motor control centers, which results in the handicap known as cerebral palsy. Because dead brain tissues cannot send messages which would normally make muscles perform smoothly, persons with cerebral palsy achieve purposeful movement only with great difficulty. Movement is jerky and without smooth uniformity for some, while others cannot walk, talk, manipulate or move at all.

Some retardates also have sight and hearing losses, and may suffer from another brain malfunction known as epilepsy, or dysrhythmia. Epilepsy has always been mysterious, but it can be rather simply defined as "an episode of the impairment of consciousness."[12] Many questions remain to be answered, especially for persons who experience the most violent kinds of seizures. Doctors now effectively use drugs in controlling these violent seizures; however, the type of epilepsy with which the Sunday school teacher usually has to cope actually has no violent aspects. Science calls it a "minor motor seizure,"[13] during which a child loses consciousness, usually losing muscle control and falling. This fall rarely harms him unless he is unusually heavy or tall, or falls against heavy or sharp objects. He slumps in a relaxed attitude, remains unconscious from fifteen to twenty seconds, and then slowly awakens to rejoin class activity.

These minor motor seizures will probably be routine occurrences in any class for trainables, and the well-adjusted teacher learns to treat them casually. He needs a basic understanding of the functioning of each child so he can properly care for him. His ability to be calm and proceed with class activity when one child has a seizure will lend needed emotional support to the rest of the students as they see the epileptic accepted in the midst of his seizures.[14]

SUMMARY

Mental retardation is the resulting condition when brain tissue does not develop properly in the prenatal stages or is destroyed during or after birth. Genetic imbalance, occurring at conception, accounts for one-third of all retardates. These children are known as Mongoloids, or are said to have Downs Syndrome. They fit into both the educable and trainable levels. Another third of all mentally handicapped persons have suffered organic or actual physical damage to the brain. This may happen due to lack of oxygen during delivery, or after birth through poisoning, accidental blows to the head, or through chemical imbalance at any stage in life.

Mentally handicapped individuals are placed into two intellectual and educational categories: The *educable* will attend special public school classes where he will learn basic fundamental skills and eventually learn enough to support himself by doing work requiring limited intellectual functioning. The *trainable* retarded, however, will probably learn those things pertaining to self-care, social habits, and his adjustment to his immediate surroundings. The IQ of a trainable retardate may be as high as 55. All retardates can and need to learn the personal love of God for them.

Retardation often involves such physical complications as slow and incomplete motor-ability development, handicapped sight and hearing, and varying degrees of cerebral palsy, as well as a mild form of epilepsy.

Since surgeons cannot yet replace brain tissue, retardation affects the entire life of an individual. The retardate's parents fear that they are the carriers of the malady, that their forefathers have borne it to them, and that they are passing it on to future generations. These fears have no basis in fact, for no one can accurately predict when conception between healthy people will result in retardation.

Professionals are fond of telling the parents, "Make his life as normal as possible." However, what is normalcy? Certainly it is a standard, but is it man's highest? Perhaps a somewhat higher standard would be to teach him to be as human as possible, which is to know one's own feelings and to establish an identity that is consistent with oneself.

2

Who Are the Trainable Mentally Retarded?

THE PROSPECTIVE TEACHER of a Sunday school class for the trainable mentally retarded visits that classroom with a multitude of questions in mind. These questions fit into three categories: What are these pupils like? How do they differ from other boys and girls? Will I be able to accept and adjust to the ways in which they differ from the norm?

Initially, the visitor goes away with many added questions, plus one other impression. He experiences a sharp emotional reaction, especially if he has never had previous contact with retarded persons. He never expected to come face to face with such an unlovely and seemingly unlovable group of children. Teachers have cautioned him to remain still and quiet, to be as unobtrusive as possible for the benefit of his own observation, and not to disturb the delicate emotional balance of the pupils.

The visitor's eyes skip from one child to another. Visually, at least, he realizes that very few generalities can be made about retarded trainables. Greta has a question mark written clearly on her face; her eyes are wrinkled in a frown. Rolypoly Ted moves sluggishly along. Fred has slanted eyes, a somewhat flattened head, a short, broad neck and a somewhat too-large tongue. Robert is handicapped with cerebral palsy, showing difficulty with purposeful movement. And Marlene shows no outward sign of retardation but is still a member of the class. There are those whose eyes look back without any response or sign of recognition — a blank gaze which may be due to impaired hearing; they see but really don't hear well or at all. Epilepsy complicates the lives of others, and one may fall limply to the floor whenever a seizure strikes him. Teachers and students alike have learned that the seizure will pass quickly. The youngster soon rouses, shakes off the effects of his short but deep sleep, and resumes the activity from which the attack took him. Newer pupils or teachers' helpers may at first be upset when such a seizure occurs, however, it becomes quite routine for the class to make allowances for the epileptic member.

A minute percentage of trainables appear nearly normal intellectually. They have been well trained in grooming and conduct, and sometimes even in their speech patterns; however, their presence in a class for trainables indicates that they cannot benefit from higher academic experience. Obviously they have made good social adjustment to retardation.

An accurate definition of the "trainable mentally retarded" (TMR) must include the perspectives of medicine, psychology, sociology, education and religion. The Sunday school teacher will need to know how the composite of these characteristics will finally affect pupil performance and potential.

Persons classified as trainables* have been defined as having IQs ranging from 30 to 55.[1] They are uneducable in terms of academic skills and will require supervision throughout their life-span. Many can learn to read signs for their own protection (such as GO, STOP, LADIES, MEN), to count and use numbers in a limited way. Their usual training program stresses primarily help in self-care, social habits, and adjustment to environment.

---

* Classifying the child as trainable according to IQ level is not without its hazards, for IQ for the trainable is not clearly defined and can range from 25-55.

PHYSICAL AND BEHAVIORAL CHARACTERISTICS

Retardation may begin in the prenatal stage of life, or in preconception in the case of hereditary deficiency.[2] It also can occur following birth as a result of disease or injury. The effects of prenatal mental deficiency make themselves felt slowly. The child grows more slowly, matures with more difficulty, and retains infant habits longer. Parents may not notice differences in a child until the time when he should begin to speak. Although slowness to speak does not indicate retardation, it can be a symptom of something serious; so it should not go unheeded. Previously the child may have seemed to be developing normally.

The clues to a child's intelligence level show up when he begins verbalizing his thoughts. Parents are alerted that something is either physically or mentally wrong when their child does not try to talk. Some doctors add to the problem by assuring the parent, "Johnny will be all right; he's just a bit slow. Come back in a year, and probably he will have snapped out of it." As a result, reality is not faced until the child is of school age.

Trainables are all physically handicapped in that their sight, hearing, speech, and general coordination have been diminished to some degree as a result of their brain injury. Such a pupil rarely speaks as naturally or as easily as a normal child because his brain does not automatically transmit the complicated signals which trigger the intricate muscle action needed for articulation. If the speech centers in his brain have indeed been extensively damaged, he will be motivated to good use of his voice only after his parents, teachers and therapists spend long hours training him in the art of communication.

Since the retardate is unlikely to ever develop a normal-sounding voice, a teacher must never criticize the sound which he makes in a genuine effort to express himself. These sounds will characteristically be of an abnormally high or monotonously low pitch, hoarse or raspy, loud or soft. The last four qualities may have their basis in permanent damage to the vocal and hearing organs. For example, the Mongoloid typically has a harsh voice with little range of pitch,[3] a verbal deficit which is due in some measure to structural defects in and around the mouth. Another child may speak loudly because he has lost some of his hearing and is raising his voice in an effort to hear himself.[4]

Some trainables use their voice regardless of the fact that no one can understand them; they are trying to communicate and make their desires known without words. Seven-year-old Tammy constantly screamed for attention because she found it to be a remarkably effective means of making her wishes known.[5] It did not necessarily imply unhappiness or displeasure, for she employed it to relate a simple request or to get permission. Teachers used a combination of discipline, praise and energy-consuming physical activity to help Tammy learn not to express herself by screaming. They expected her to progress slowly, and she did. One of her teachers explains the kind of attitude which is necessary when dealing with the trainable and his behavioral problems:

> I couldn't take the noise away from Tammy, but she herself stopped it when she could beat on the drum and participate in large muscle activities with the more mature pupils in class. We must have the stability not to take away what the children bring to us, whether it is destructive or not. We must accept them where they are and turn them toward constructive behavior. Before you can take anything away, you should have something with which to replace it.[6]

Some Christian educators in the field of retardation do not feel that children with extreme behavioral problems should be enrolled in a regular Sunday school class until their behavior has been modified in special education classes or at home. However, when Sunday school teachers have special training to handle the retarded, the child may receive the help he needs in class.

Trainables often use reactionary behavior because, as illustrated above, no one ever helped them to learn a different mode of communication. A pupil may become aggressive, hostile, or withdrawn when he fails in efforts to express himself. Some trainables, such as those who cannot hear, simply retreat and isolate themselves. Teachers can often break the hostility of the nearly deaf child, as well as those who cannot talk, by making sure that he understands, by teaching him to control his own emotions when he does not understand, and by including him in everything. Teachers can use visual materials to minimize a hearing deficit and also aid nonverbal students in understanding a given lesson. This helps their understanding through the use of their senses. He not only uses abundant visual aids, but can embrace the children and give further physical reinforcement, such as helping their hands to perform a task. The teacher uses his eyes to express approval. Trainables whose behavior tends to be loud and disruptive can become acceptable for classroom activity if they can be taught to respond to efforts to modify their actions.[7]

The teacher will see vast differences in the body size and shape of trainables, for they inherit physical qualities just as everyone else, but various studies show that they tend to be somewhat smaller in size than the norm. Howe and Smith indicate that growth rates are usually slower, accounting for a generally shorter stature and lighter physique.[8] Some have growth abnormalities, such as in height and obesity. In addition, there are dazed conditions, odd body and facial mannerisms, excessive fondling of others and unusual emotional states.[9]

Behavioral characteristics of Mongoloids are not as distinctive as their physical characteristics, however, certain generalities have been made.[10] In infancy many tend to be placid and inert, although some are restless and constantly grimacing. Sitting up, walking and talking are all markedly delayed. Attracted by everything around them, they are observant and alert-appearing. They show aptness for mimicry, may have a marked sense of rhythm, and are especially fond of music.

Teachers must be especially alert for the seemingly normal-looking child. Jenny, who was enrolled in a Sunday school class for trainables, gave the impression that she had a much greater intelligence than in reality she possessed. Extensive testing had failed to place her any higher, yet she had a clean, neat, and hardly unusual appearance. She had gained enough sophistication to make her acceptable in a group, provided she did not try to compete conversationally. In class she thoroughly enjoyed the use of a workbook, which stemmed from the fact that she attended a private school where teachers placed a high value on good penmanship. She copied every word beautifully, but she had no actual understanding of the things she was writing. Nevertheless, she found intense satisfaction and pride in her writing activities. Teachers soon realized that they could demand no more of Jenny than of other class members.

The role of the Sunday school teacher of retardates is to develop an awareness of the love of God and of His discipline in the life of the pupil. He desires to teach the retarded child how to respond in a way which will please the heavenly Father, by means of his senses, feeling the love of his teachers, catching the attitude of reverence, and touching and smelling the wonders of creation. In the process, the teacher works as closely with him as does any other adult in his life, exerting extensive influence upon his personality development — influence either positive or negative, constructive or destructive, but never neutral. Trainable pupils lack both the reasoning power and emotional stability to act positively upon a negative reaction by their teacher, thus researchers have suggested several principles from which to guide personality development:[11]

1. Positive reinforcement will increase the possible occurrence of a particular behavioral reaction. For example, one Sunday's lesson is to teach pupils how to participate in the worship service, and two boys have been assigned to take the offering. One pupil in the "congregation" decides to keep the basket when it is passed by him, an "usher" tries to retrieve it by force, and a fight begins. The teacher needs the almost impossible ability to calmly stop the fight without showing negative emotions toward anyone involved. He pleasantly takes the basket from the offender and, in the process of returning it to the usher, lavishes praise upon him for his work. The teacher admonishes the other boy in positive terms: "We do it this way, Larry; pass the basket on." Proclaiming Larry a "bad boy" in front of the class would only degrade his self-image.

2. More praise than punishment should be meted out.

3. The reinforcement should be as immediate as possible. That is, immediately try to show each boy the ways in which he did the right thing. Use a smile, a caress, or other simple rewards which seem pleasurable to the child. Teachers need much ingenuity in discovering reinforcements which work with individual pupils, for this will be one of their most crucial teaching tools.

4. Whenever possible, verbalize the reinforcements. "Put your money in the offering basket, Kathy," the teacher encourages as he physically helps the reluctant child to release the coins. He continues, "That's the way we do it. You're learning well."

5. Be consistent in applying positive and negative reinforcements. Teachers, like everyone else, sometimes show inconsistency. This occurs most often on those days which we call "bad days," when physical and emotional stamina ebbs. Occasionally teachers will be tempted to handle the above-

described incident by grabbing the basket from Larry and looking back at him in definite disapproval. Every class member senses when his teacher is upset. Thus the whole class becomes disturbed because a trainable has nothing within himself to balance the effect of someone else's troubled spirit. A teacher must never allow a trainable to do something he has previously forbidden him to do, for the child will only become more deeply confused.

6. Positive reinforcement should be administered to the child, regardless of whether it is specific to the behavior he is displaying. The child is told he is doing a good job when coloring a paper, even when he should be coloring in the book.

Verbalized reinforcement is insufficient in itself, so the teacher must use tangible objects. For example, the lavish use of bright-colored stickers, such as stars, goes a long way with the young trainable. One little girl looked up into the sky and said to her teacher, "Look at the beautiful sticker." The teacher then sang, "Twinkle, twinkle, little sticker. How I wonder how you flicker." Animal stickers are equally useful, for with each sticker the child can be urged to make the sound of the animal, or to perform its movements.

Certain behavioral characteristics displayed by the trainable may be signals to the teacher that he is crying for attention and reassurance, and perhaps even for discipline. Baumgartner lists some of these signs:[12]

Fearfulness — The child may be tense and unable to relax and participate in group activities.

Destructive drives — This child may never have succeeded at any kind of task. In frustration he destroys things.

Mistrust of adults — Especially if no one in their home has ever tried to love, understand and guide them, these children may mistrust adults. Those coming to Sunday school from an institutional life will also display this mistrust, for the staff in a home for the mentally retarded, especially a public home, is rarely large enough to give children personalized care.

Withdrawal, showing anxiety, and no signs of happy, contented feelings (such as a smile), and crying or screaming loudly may also point up the pupil's need.

The teacher will be faced with the job of modifying or changing these tendencies in the pupil. Not only will the pupil be a socially better person if he succeeds; probably he will also be able to experience God's love simply because someone cared enough to help him cope with his problems.

In modifying behavior, the teacher chooses an activity which a pupil can carry through successfully, and which is also designed to replace the need for his undesirable actions, tantrums, withdrawal, and other symptoms. However, the staff must choose modification techniques carefully and with a specific child in mind. For example, two trainable pupils were set to work at the same table on a finger-painting project. One child showed a happy, satisfied attitude as he worked, but the other child had a tantrum and began shouting and destructively scattering materials about. An analysis of the situation revealed these facts: The child who worked contentedly possessed good finger coordination and so felt accomplished and fulfilled by the painting session. The other child was handicapped by cerebral palsy, and his frustration welled up when his fingers would not cooperate with what he wanted to do. He displayed his feelings of defeat and misery in the form of destruction — something at which he could succeed.[13]

Social and Emotional Characteristics

In social adjustment the trainable retardate faces the most crucial and difficult part of his life because our social structure tends to filter out those who deviate from the norm, and trainable retardates are admittedly different. "Unfinished children," "an interesting process," and "defective" are ways in which society views the retarded, with whom they feel socially ill-at-ease. The curious thing is that trainables have emotional needs similar to those of the normal person, but those needs are intensified.

Studies of the social and emotional adjustments of the trainable show significant differences in the one-to-one situation. They respond slowly and only after long periods of learning to trust a teacher, and they deviate from other children in a social situation through hyperactivity and tantrums, ignoring commands, and destroying their own clothing.[14] Goldberg lists (in rank order) problems of the trainable retarded as found in reports from 85 teachers on 1,200 children in special classes:

1. Shy, fearful, tense
2. Hyperactive, nervous
3. Attention-seeker
4. Short attention span
5. Stubborn, obstinate
6. Poor communication
7. Poor motor ability
8. Mischievous, destructive
9. Aggressive
10. Emotionally unstable
11. Withdrawn
12. Infantile, immature
13. Annoying and undesirable habits
14. Selfish, egotistical
15. Not dependable
16. Socially incompetent
17. Perseverates[15]

This list of characteristics primarily reveals the extent and strength of the retardates' negative and destructive tendencies, which should make the teacher realize just how desperately these children need guidance in constructive emotional behavior. Some parents have not provided this guidance; instead they feel strongly compelled to suppress the retardate's aggressive behavior because society seems intolerant and fearful of his tantrums.[16] Of course, parents cannot expect the Sunday school to enroll and handle their undisciplined child, but the staff should plan strategy to use during displays of hostility or restlessness. They must know how to channel hostile energy into an activity which will use it up and at the same time build the retardate's ego.[17]

One Sunday morning a class of retarded children became restless during storytime, an indication to the teacher that they had to spend their energy before they would settle down once again and listen. "She quietly picked up a small drum and began to tap it. One child got out of his chair and the others followed. They moved about the room."[18] She beat the drum louder, and their movements became larger and noisier until all were stamping and throwing their bodies into the movement. The teacher passed the drum to one of the boys, who changed the rhythm to a staccato beat. The class reacted by jumping. Soon the teacher retrieved the instrument and gradually slowed and softened the beat. Stopping the music, she quietly asked the children to take their seats and then gave them time to catch their breath. With tensions gone, she resumed the storytime.

The severely retarded has other social needs in addition to the need for abundant emotional support. He wants to be an acceptable member of his Sunday school class, but this depends upon how well teachers provide him with constant supervision. He cannot accept unsupervised responsibility because he has great difficulty in developing consistent behavior patterns, but the socially adjusted trainable readily responds when adults give him a direction or order. He is teacher-motivated rather than self-motivated, but teacher-motivation only succeeds in an atmosphere where the pupil feels a bond of friendship with his teacher. Through friendship she can inspire him to imitate her actions.

Consider the example of trainables learning to collect the

musical instruments after a rhythm-band session. The teacher, who is always methodical, deliberate, direct and kind, rises, selects a pupil, takes him by the hand and says, "Roger, please collect the instruments." Her speech is simple; her language clear. The teacher leads Roger step by step in the initial learning process, perhaps helping those who are reluctant to give up their instruments and then placing the instruments in Roger's hands. A teacher may have to repeat this process numerous times before class members will carry through with a simple direction from her, and some pupils will never succeed.

LEARNING CHARACTERISTICS

Learning characteristics of the trainable retarded pupil not only have their basis in mental deficiency, for the injury which resulted in retardation also affected the brain's motor centers to varying degrees. The child is intellectually unable to send the proper messages to the motor centers of his brain. Damage to brain centers prevents the message from affecting the muscle control which is found in a normal child. The retarded pupil has yet another handicap; he sees that he does not perform as well as other people, and this may make him emotionally upset.

Retardates at the trainable level have learning difficulties and deficiencies in the following areas:

Drive and ambition
Creativity and originality
Imagination
Initiative, curiosity, high standards of workmanship
Powers of concentration, extended attention span except
under the most ideal learning conditions
Quick reaction to stimuli
Completing tasks
Setting goals and long-term plans
Following subsequent directions
Sensitivity to detail

Detecting error and absurdities
Recognizing familiar elements in new situations, forming
analogies
Judging, organizing, evaluating
Drawing on past experience to solve problems
Gaining, utilizing concepts
Dealing, thinking abstractly
Problem-solving, critical-thinking, decision-making
Using language effectively
Associating words with ideas[19]

Some of the difficulties listed above can be attributed to
the fact that the trainable retardate has extremely poor reasoning ability.[20] Thus the degree with which it will handicap
his everyday life will depend upon the amount of reasoning
involved and the complexity and abstractness of a given task.
Also, the retardate cannot judge the quality of his own product
without these reasoning powers.[21]

SUMMARY

The characteristics of the trainable mentally retarded
child include many generalities. These are noted to show how
he differs from a normal person. However, his teacher must
deal with him as an individual, and meet his needs from an
inventive point of view. The technique which works with one
child may not be effective or may have a harmful effect on
another pupil. The Sunday school teacher should concentrate
on the child's moral and spiritual needs, but in doing so he
must pay continual attention to his limited learning ability and
make specific compensations through effective teaching methods.

Retardation becomes evident at the age when a child
normally begins to speak. Intelligence tests will place him at
the level of the trainable when his IQ falls between 30 and
55. He will benefit from home and school training which does
not require academic subjects. Approximately 25 percent of

all known trainables hold some kind of job, but they work only under highly supervised conditions.

Body size and shape (including height) differ, so that a trainable retardate cannot be identified on that basis alone. Many are physically handicapped in numerous and varying ways, but none will have the same combination of handicaps as another.

Every trainable shows emotional and social imbalance through displays of negative personality traits; he reacts negatively because the damaged brain tissue inhibits more positive responses. Since nothing can make the intelligence centers healthy and functional once again, the retardate will not like nor accept himself unless he has been extremely well trained and deeply loved at home. He only knows that he cannot act and react in the same way as those surrounding him.

He also shows primary negative learning characteristics. The teacher can modify these traits and motivate the child toward more acceptable behavior. Finally, he has at least two normal drives. He needs love and security. Also he has the capacity to feel that God is love and that He cares for him.

3

How Do the Mentally Retarded Learn?

TEENAGED ANITA bore the social poise of many other teenagers in her church. She had a friendly attitude and interest in people, so she could greet visitors and make them feel comfortable. In addition, she had a definite flair for grooming and dressed neatly. She even spoke with a certain sophistication and authority.

Despite all this, Anita enrolled in a Sunday school class for trainables, for she had the mentality of a beginner child. Furthermore, she fit into the retarded class immediately and with ease. The casual observer might wonder why Anita needed to be in a special class, but there was little doubt by her teachers that her knowledge was not the product of her own thinking. Having picked up certain facts and concepts through memory, she was able to repeat them in a convincing manner; but tests of her mental capacity actually showed that her intelligence fell to the level of the trainable retarded.

Certain characteristics about Anita demonstrate that trainables do learn, and she further exemplifies that they also have need of teaching in the spiritual realm. One Sunday morning before class had begun, the teachers found Anita embracing another girl in an obvious effort to comfort her, for both were crying and speaking to each other in solicitous tones.

Other pupils explained that the two girls had begun an energetic fight, kicking and swinging at each other. But suddenly at one point in the squabble, Anita began to feel sorry that she had attacked her friend. Coming upon the scene at just that moment, the teachers found Anita praying, with hands folded and eyes turned toward heaven, "O God, please forgive me." They also observed a look of terror in the girl's eyes, which strengthened their knowledge that she had learned the difference between doing the right thing and the wrong thing.

The term *learning* should be defined as a basis on which to begin a discussion of how the trainable retarded learn. Melton describes it as "a change in behavior naturally correlated with experience or training, occurring when a person must react to a situation for which his previously acquired modes of response are inadequate, and it is therefore essentially a process of adjustment to satisfy a need or motive."[1] In other words, a person reacts to meet a new need. At this point we can differentiate between learning in the mentally retarded and learning in the normal child.

Trainables are first of all, persons, and second, trainable persons. They must be treated as human beings and be respected as they are taught. Learning must take place where they are. The Sunday school teacher will have to use much repetition in his teaching, for the trainable must repeatedly practice even minor things before he can perform well. A single performance or a one-time story is of little value to him. Moreover, he cannot draw conclusions from his experiences. Methods that demand mobility of mind are unsuitable for use with the retarded. He cannot recognize relationships or make connections, nor can he draw analogies. When the Sunday school teacher asks a question, the retarded pupil will respond immediately, because he feels that to answer promptly gives the best satisfaction.

Trainables rarely learn to tell time accurately because the thinking process requires a rational building of fact on fact: the little hand is on two, the big hand is on three, therefore, it is 2:15. Trainables cannot grasp the abstract meaning of numbers, and thus cannot come to the deductive conclusion involved in telling time.

When no logical, reasoning, thought-building process is involved in a learning procedure, the trainable pupil will likely succeed if all other positive factors, such as a comfortable, secure environment, and approving and undemanding teachers have been provided. In fact, the retarded can succeed and sometimes excel at tasks which they can learn by rote.[2] Baumeister encourages the teacher by pointing out that continued practice in motor learning seems to be basic to all development — as speech and balance — and leads into the basic concepts upon which children build ideas sequentially.[3] Through practice he seems to improve at a faster rate than normals, and he can sustain that rate over a longer period of time. Teachers should capifalize on this by training students to do routine tasks which are a regular part of class activities, such as distributing materials, and setting up the room for various activities. Baumeister further describes the success of this method known as *conditioning:* "The frequency of desired response is subject to the pleasant consequences of that response. That is, teachers must be prepared to reward the student who has successfully completed a task with something pleasurable, even her own smile. No endeavor can go unrecognized."[4]

Studies have shown that the teacher who gives approval which trainables can both see and feel, will not only be helping them to learn, but may actually be serving to boost their intelligence levels.

Rothstein sums up the research into the learning ability of the mentally retarded as a group by succinctly stating, "Their learning will primarily be at the habit-forming level."[5] Trainables do not benefit from the spontaneous kinds of learning experiences through which the normal student picks up a great deal of knowledge; the normal student can logically relate one situation to another, and thus applies known principles to new experiences.

The retardate does not possess this ability to transfer knowledge. But because he has the capability of feeling the same fears, hopes and frustrations as anyone else, he is painfully aware that his performance falls behind that of other people, and particularly normal children in his own age group. However, the mentally alert person brings his powers of rationality to do the work of compensating for his fears and frustrations. Conversely, the retarded student becomes altogether defenseless without the use of these compensating powers in a learning situation, especially if teachers have failed to specifically structure the situation to give him a feeling of accomplishment.[6]

A great deal of learning success achieved by the retardate does depend upon his teacher's insight and planning for his problems. The teacher's knowledge of the circumstances under which the child performs best, may lead to more effective means of training and educating him.[7] If he were always able to determine the specific deficits or handicaps in any one case, he might be able to minimize these handicaps through adjustment. This adjustment will take many forms. First of all, the child must be comfortable. Perhaps this means that, initially, he will need the total attention of his teacher in a secluded part of the room. The teacher then encounters a communication barrier if a child has sensory losses. Can he hear, see and speak well enough to begin receiving instruction? The teacher has several alternatives when he faces the problem of communicating with the trainable pupil. He can be instructed by a professional therapist to help him reach the child, although he must never actually play the role of therapist. He can at least gain an understanding of the problem.

Second, a teacher may want to permit an uncommunicative pupil to remain in class and participate in his own limited way as long as he does not disrupt general activity. Teachers should probably allow the docile child to remain, since no one can finally measure the kinds of benefits he receives from a class. Finally, teachers must refuse to enroll the trainable child whose hyperactive temperament turns a class to chaos.

Another adjustment concerns language. A teacher must be overly conscious that learning success in mentally retarded students depends upon his ability to speak in words and terms which they understand. He must begin at the language level of his students, work at that level, and then slowly introduce new words.[*] He should select and introduce new words on the basis of their usefulness to the retardate.[8] This especially applies to the retardate and religious concepts. Such words as *love, helping, serving, sadness,* and *hurt* will give the retardate something which he can understand. The higher theological terms which have no basis in sight, feeling or touch will have little meaning to him.

---

[*] Teachers in the special Sunday school class may be surprised to hear pupils repeating words and ideas which they later come to see have no meaning to those pupils. Teachers must be careful to abandon everyday Christian jargon if they are really serious about aiding the spiritual needs of the mentally retarded.

4

Is Salvation for the Mentally Retarded?

INTERPRETATIONS OF RELIGIOUS CONSCIOUSNESS
THE RELIGIOUS AWARENESS of the retarded has been approached in various ways. Some deny both the presence of religious consciousness and the ability of the retarded to be saved, a denial which puts the retarded somewhere below the level of human beings. Martin Luther referred to the feeble-minded as "godless" and reported the following occurrence in one of his Table Talks:

> Eight years ago, there was one [feebleminded] at Dessau whom I, Martinus Luther, saw and grappled with. He was twelve years old, had the use of his eyes and all his senses, so that one might think that he was a normal child. But he did nothing but gorge himself, as much as four pheasants or threshers. He ate, defecated and drooled and if anyone tackled him, he screamed. If things didn't go well, he wept. So I said to the Prince of Anhalt: "If I were the Prince, I should take this child to the Moldau River which flows near Dessau and drown him." But the Prince of Anhalt and the Prince of Savony, who happened to be present, refused to follow my advice. Thereupon I said: "Well, then the Christians shall order the Lord's Prayer to be said in church and pray that the dear Lord take the Devil away." This was done daily in Dessau and the changeling died in the following year. When Luther was asked why he had made such a recommendation, he replied that he was firmly of the opinion that such change-

38

lings were merely a mass of flesh, a *massa carnis,* with no soul. For it is the Devil's power that he corrupts people who have reason and souls when he possesses them. The Devil sits in such changelings where their soul should have been.[1]

Emil Brunner, who contends that the mentally retarded are without the image of God, says that the *imago dei* is basically centered in responsibility. Man's response to God may be, "I do not know any creator, and I will not obey any God." If this is an answer, it comes under the inherent law of responsibility. "It is identical with human existence as such, and indeed with the quality of being which all human beings possess equally; it only ceases where true human living ceases, on the borderline of imbecility or madness."[2]

Some take the stand that the retarded are "heaven's very special children," or more than human, the instruments of God for a very special mission.[3] The authors, in teaching trainable mentally retarded persons, would be very reluctant to ignore their right to basic human nature, for it is constantly evident. In fact, Seguin recognized this in his early approaches to the mentally retarded: "That the idiot is endowed with a moral nature, no one who has had the happiness of ministering to him will deny."[4] Sister Mary Theodore very aptly describes the view of the authors at this point when she says that sometimes the retarded are called "eternal children,"[5] but this kind of label denies their ability for social development.

The Lutheran position attributes both religious consciousness and responsibility to the mentally retarded, a position based on the belief that the Word of God does not excuse the child from the guilt of original inherited sin which corrupts the entire human race. The exceptional child, like all infants, needs a Saviour from sin.[6]

Another approach concedes religious consciousness but denies religious responsibility,[7] a view which recognizes that retarded persons are aware of religion and perhaps even find in it a quiet solace, but there is no responsibility, nor do they take religious commitments seriously. In fact, responsibility per se is denied by this position. "Similarly, a church member excused the behavior of two retarded adolescents observed kissing each other during the church service by saying that 'they are not responsible.' However, only a few weeks previously she had voted, along with the rest of the church, to approve these two as candidates for believers' baptism."

The authors believe that even as children of normal intelligence receive recognition as responsible persons by degrees only and not in totality, so also the mentally retarded should be treated similarly with regard to religious responsibility. Stubblefield agrees by stating, "Religious consciousness and responsibility are relative to mental and chronological development."[9] Sister Mary Theodore concurs:

> Intelligence is a factor in an individual's responsibility for his moral behavior. The moral responsibility of extremely retarded individuals presents no problem. A child with a mental age of less than three years can have no clear concept of right and wrong. A severely retarded individual, with mental age from three to seven, has a limited concept of the goodness or wickedness of an act. He is capable of some moral training, but the degree of responsibility is small. He cannot have sufficient reflection, and he fails to see the implications of his action and to foresee consequences. The severely retarded individual lacks the insight needed for serious responsibility and frequently acts without thought of anything beyond the immediate present.[10]

The limitations of the retarded must be realistically accepted, and they are judged on the basis of their knowledge and understanding, which avoids the tendency to pronounce categorical judgments without personal involvement with the trainable retarded.

The preceding conclusions constitute the basis upon which a sound ministry of Christian education for the mentally handicapped can be based. However, a congregation should first have full understanding of its moral and spiritual responsibility to the retarded, and thus the authors refer interested persons to specific sources.[11]

Religious Concepts of the Trainable Mentally Retarded

Much more needs to be researched on the religious concepts which can be grasped by trainable retardates, for they deserve to be understood within their own conceptual framework. Educators do have some information from which to work, such as Oliver Graebner's study on the "God concept."[12] His instrument, which contained twenty-two drawings from life situations with questions, was administered to 398 retarded persons in a church-related institution, and to 467 retarded persons in publicly supported institutions in thirteen states. A number of concluding observations were made:

1. Mentally retarded people in public and church-related institutions acquire much religious conceptual framework, reflecting in the main, many of the basic ideas of the Christian religion in our culture.

2. In general, those with higher mental ability receive and reflect more conceptual sophistication.

3. Males responded somewhat stronger than females.

4. At a church-related institution, special religious instruction (e.g., confirmation instruction) seems to pay off in stronger religious frames of references, greater facility in religious language.

5. Individual differences exist at all levels of age and mental level and in various institutions.

6. Due to the limited sample at most state schools participating in the study, all responses from retarded in state schools were treated as one population; there was no separation of data by schools.

7. The order of strength of conceptual understanding at the church-related institution was as follows: Omnipresence, Omniscience, Mercy, Creator; and at the state insti-

tution: Omniscience, Promise-keeper, Mercy, Creator-Preserver, Mercy-Love-Helper.

8. Religious concepts which yielded the lowest scores included the series of ideas regarding time, angels, and justice.

9. The picture-and-question combination probably helped many respondents steer fairly clear of obvious anthropomorphizing, although there were instances of this kind of response at various points in the administration.[13]

Stubblefield, who studied general religious concepts of thirty-six institutionalized retarded persons at Clover Bottom Hospital and School, Donelson, Tennessee, found mental age to be the most significant factor in levels of religious conceptualization. The quality and number of the religious concepts of the retardates whose IQ score fell below 30 were extremely limited, while the religious concepts of the trainable retardates had a more sophisticated quality and were more numerous. There was little ability to conceptualize abstract theological beliefs. In contrast to those with an IQ below 30, all of the trainable retardates conceptualized religious ideas.[14]

The writers concur with Stubblefield's research results. In primary research with trainable retarded females at Klingberg School, Home and Treatment Center, whose chronological ages ranged from ten to thirty-seven, their concepts of God, Jesus, the Holy Spirit, the church, missions, sin and salvation were probed.*

Mental age was found to be the most significant factor in the levels of religious conceptualization. Concerning God, one

---

* The Klingberg School is approved by the Department of Mental Health of the State of Illinois. Its purpose is to provide home care as well as educational instruction. Residents include both male and female retarded of all etymolgical classifications and levels of learning, ranging from the very young (six) to the elderly. This school is not church-related but has a distinctive Christian atmosphere. The daily program, in addition to providing educational instruction, is designed to make each resident feel at ease as a member of a group and to furnish suitable recreation, and to inculcate an appreciation of the spiritual concept as well. One of the authors, Mrs. Groff, was a member of the teaching staff, 1967-68.

trainable retardate of twenty-four years with an IQ of 49 said, "God is a Supreme Being, who knows all things, can do all things, and is most perfect because he hasn't had a sin."† Another lady with a CA of thirty-seven, MA of six years and an IQ of 46 said, "God is a spirit, He saves people. If there is any troubles we should talk to the Lord about it." Some responded to the God concept by saying that He is in heaven. One girl, CA of fourteen, IQ of 30, said that God is Jesus and He made the "sun, sky, tree." Three of the group (eleven total) confused God with Jesus. Generally, God was conceived in anthropomorphic terms, such as being a person who could help you and can do many things.

Most of these trainable retardates conceptualized Jesus as the Son of God who gives protection and help to us. The girl with an IQ of 49 said, "He is three persons in one. He sits up on his throne and watches us all day and all night." One girl (IQ of 44) considered His works: "He works miracles. We love Him because He made us." One unique student, IQ of 33, had this to say: "Jesus is Son of God. Made people well. He helped them in wheel chair. He cleaned our hearts so there was no black stuff on it. He went to heaven to be with God." An emotionally disturbed twenty-four-year-old girl with an IQ of 30 said, "Jesus is in heaven. He prays. He died on the cross on Easter. He rose again." A girl with an IQ of 41 said, "Jesus is the Son of God. He talks to people. He gave us food and place to live. He slept in stable when he was little boy. He died for our sins." Another (IQ of 46) said: "Jesus was crucified for our sins."

The Holy Spirit was generally not understood. Several said you cannot see Him, but most had no answer or claimed He was God, Jesus or the Holy Ghost.

In agreement with the religious concepts of the five-year-old mental group, these girls identified the church with defi-

---

† This student, prior to coming to Klingberg School, was taught religion in a Catholic school.

nite religious activities: "We learn about God," "sing," "We go to worship," "We pray and play in church." One retardate defined it in terms of its equipment: "stained-glass windows, seats to sit down, and a lot of people singing." Two of the older retardates identified missionaries as "someone who tells others about God." The others had no concept of missionaries, except for one Catholic retardate who identified them with priests.

Concerning sin, most of the subjects considered it "real bad." One (IQ of 33) verbalized: "Sin is called real bad and that's why we have Jesus, because He cleans our heart." Another said, "Sin is very bad thing that leads you and God takes away. He died on cross to take our sins away." Most other answers resembled these.

When asked what being "saved" or "salvation" was, various responses were given. Some referred to it as literal salvation, such as being spared from a car accident. One subject had no response, and a sampling of other responses follows:

"When you die you go up to be with the Lord. If they believe God then they be with Him and if they don't they go underground."

"Save us from our sins by asking Jesus for forgiveness. If they believe in Jesus they go to heaven."

"It means the Son of God does save you from sins. Jesus has saved your life."

One Catholic expressed it this way: "Saved means go to Confession."

On the basis of this study, several conclusions can be drawn. First, trainable mentally retarded persons have a religious consciousness and awareness which they are able to conceptualize. The authors are aware that the mentally retarded may be parroting adult speech, but day-to-day contact makes them believe the level of understanding was significant and that there was conceptualization. *As mental age increases, the ability to conceptualize religious experiences also increases.*

The concepts of the trainable mentally retarded tend to be related to actual life situations; however, as mental age rises, their concepts become more abstract. But the majority of the trainable mentally retarded will never reach the abstract level of thinking. The church must build its program of religious education on this basic fact.

As noted, religious consciousness is relative to mental age. One subject studied had an IQ of 22 and could not conceptualize any religious knowledge. Since trainable retardates relate religious concepts to their own interpersonal situations, the paramount consideration is not whether they have religious consciousness and responsibility, but rather, to what degree their knowledge and responsibility extend.

When presenting salvation to the mentally retarded, use the plan of salvation found in Scripture, for the road to salvation is open to the trainable, and the road is constructed in such a way that they, too, can travel it. However, since they have childlike understanding, use a childlike approach with them.

First, the retardate, like any other person, should understand that he is a sinner in God's sight: "For all have sinned and come short of the glory of God" (Ro 3:23). A person must know of his need for salvation before he is motivated to seek God's forgiveness. Second, the penalty of sin is taught in the Scripture: "The wages of sin is death, but the gift of God is eternal life through Jesus Christ our Lord" (Ro 6:23). The retardate's less-sophisticated understanding of sin does not mean God can "overlook" the punishment of that sin because if he has an awareness of sin, he is guilty before God and must do something about the sin question. Christ is the answer. However, the retardate who is unable to conceptualize a religious experience and has no knowledge of right and wrong cannot be held accountable. Third, God has provided a substitute for sin. The retarded who has enough comprehension to be responsible for his sin, has enough mental ability to understand that "Christ died for him." He may not understand all the implications of atonement, but he can comprehend that Christ died for his sin. "But God commendeth his love toward us, in that, while we were yet sinners, Christ died for us" (Ro 5:8).

Finally, the retarded who has sufficient comprehension, as with all persons, must respond in a personal way, making a simple volitional act of faith. This step of commitment for salvation is called "trusting in Jesus," "receiving Jesus Christ into the life," or personal faith. Both phrases describe the act of becoming a Christian, and the mentally retarded who has the mental ability to recognize he is a sinner can receive Jesus Christ into his life. "But as many as received him, to them gave he power to become the sons of God, even to them that believe on his name" (Jn 1:12).

Some educators disagree with the presentation of salvation to a mentally retarded person, claiming that evangelists are manipulating them to make a decision. However, if the retarded has passed the age of accountability, the consequences are too great not to present salvation. For even though some mentally retarded person may on occasion be manipulated into a meaningless "profession of faith," there have been a number who have made intelligent decisions for God; therefore, the authors favor presenting Jesus Christ to the retarded and asking them to make a decision for salvation.

PART II

Successful Ministry

5

What Church Program Should Be Used?

A LARGE EAST COAST CHURCH discovered that it had many persons in its midst who had been labeled "trainable" (TMR).* Five families in the congregation had one child or adult living at home whose handicaps included TMR. The public schools provided classes for these children, but no church in this city of 100,000 offered them Christian teaching. Many more families, therefore, might be candidates for evangelism and church attendance if they knew a church which had a program for the trainables.

This church established a Christian education class for trainable retarded pupils, but unknowingly, the Christian education board placed the class in a less-than-ideal setting: the basement room occupied by the heating system. At face value, the advantages seemed to be there. The room was a secluded, private area away from outside noise and distractions, well heated, and free of bright decor and decoration which tend to excite the trainable individual.

Except for warmth, this class could hardly have been placed in a worse environment. The room was located in a remote part of the building, so most retarded pupils would be unable to make their way through the maze of stairways and corridors leading to class, and thus parents could not allow them to find their way alone.

Nevertheless, parents did bring these children to church

---

* Person whose IQ falls below 55.

faithfully, because here the family could all attend services together. None had to stay home and baby-sit with the retardate. This church cared enough to serve the entire family, inadequate as the facilities seemed to be.

A church in California possessed this same kind of vision to evangelize the mentally retarded and their families. But the church's board members had an added dimension to their spiritual vision, for they realized that the special environmental needs of the TMR must be met before teachers could succeed in providing purposeful learning experiences. The special education room in the new building of the church offered these advantages: planners located it on the ground floor with an entrance directly off from the parking lot. No steps impeded the pupils' ability to enter the room with ease.

The pupil entered a subtly lighted and comfortable room, with shades at the windows and nonglaring color scheme which teachers had designed to appeal and yet not to excite him. Lining two walls were closed cabinets where teachers kept all books and supplies. Except for the bulletin board where teachers displayed some of the pupils' own work, no paraphernalia lay around. Movable room dividers gave teachers the opportunity to use many types of groupings. The custodian had assured that the room would always have a warm, even temperature and be free from drafts, and the room had an adequate ventilating system. Washrooms opened onto the classroom; each including two sizes of toilets.

The congregation of the Northeast Assembly of God in Portland, Oregon, responded kindly when a family with a Mongoloid boy joined their church, even though there were times when his actions were embarrassing.[1] The people grew in their understanding and sympathy for the mentally retarded when a second young man began attending. Timmy Sumner, a fifteen-year-old Mongoloid, became the third mentally retarded child to attend. Because there was no special Sunday school class, Timmy was placed in the teen class, where the high school youths' love for Timmy made allowance for his disturbance.

"But we had to do something," said the Rev. Larry Steller, the church's minister. Learning that there was no sponsored school for mentally retarded in the Greater Portland area, a weekday school was begun in the church basement with eighteen enrolled. It was given the name "Timmy School."

Timmy Sumner, for whom the school is named, is a friend to all, both young and old. A close companion called him "a kind of mascot in our congregation." Everybody knows of Timmy's love for the Lord, and the high schoolers show their acceptance by taking Timmy on overnight retreats.

The enthusiasm of Timmy School was contagious. A Sunday school class for the mentally retarded was inaugurated. Using a regular primary class quarterly with laymen teaching, they reached more mentally retarded children.

When Reverend Steller was asked what the ministry to the retarded children has done for his church, he replied, "Our community knows we care, because the Lord's concern for people is translated into action."

A new $150,000 unit was constructed for the week-long ministry. Timmy School has also helped change the educational methodology of the church. "No more small Sunday School rooms for us," stated Steller, "but large multi-purpose rooms which will be used for team teaching on Sunday and the rest of the week for a new enlarged Timmy School program."

Other results are evident through the church's outreach. One girl was admitted back into high school and three others were received into Portland grade schools after having been in Timmy School.

Steller lists encouragement to parents as a final contribution of the ministry to mentally retarded. "God has worked in the hearts of parents, helping them accept their children's handicap." He mentioned evangelistic outreach as a second benefit to the program: "They can be converted the same as other children." Steller added, "Several mentally retarded children were converted last year."

These examples illustrate the fact that effective Christian education for TMR persons depends upon careful organization and administration of the program. In beginning such a ministry, churches are commonly faced with at least three problems which involve the relation of the special program to the total church program, the management of retarded persons in existing programs, and the creation of a special class or department.[2]

One of the first steps toward organizing a special class is homogeneous grouping;[3] in other words, due to differences of intellectual ability and social interests, all mentally retarded persons could not receive maximum benefit by being classed together. Neither could the teacher be as effective as with a homogeneous group.

Classes for the trainable mentally retarded should be structured by five criteria:[4] chronological age,† and the physical, mental, social and emotional needs.‡[5]

Educable Pupils in Existing Programs

Educable mentally handicapped students can be placed

---

† The National Council of Churches has developed a curriculum plan that includes a series for trainables and another for the educable. Each series is divided into three chronological age groups (for the trainable, 6-10, 11-15, 16-21; and for the educable, 7-12, 13-16, 17-25). Sections of the material for the trainable, to be published by the Cooperative Publication Association, were available for use in late 1969 or early 1970. The teaching-learning units are "experience oriented." They are flexibly designed for use in the local church, institutions, culturally deprived sections where retardation seems to be a cultural-familial phenomenon, and sheltered workshops.

‡ He needs food, clothing and shelter. He also needs physical, mental and social stimuli if he is to reach his full potential. Other needs include love, acceptance, discipline, opportunity to develop, to have identity and exercise creativity. In addition to what has been mentioned, the retarded person needs to learn how to live successfully with peers who are more able in many areas than he is. He needs social contacts with others in a group. Each retarded person needs opportunity to contribute to the happiness and welfare of others, to know that he has a contribution to make.

within the regular departments of the Sunday school, for they are usually accepted in the public school special education classes where teachers would not be allowed to enroll them if they had not already reached certain levels of good social behavior. In addition, they need the emotional stimulation and secure feeling of being with their own age group. Thus it is a healthy thing for the educable retardate if his church makes a place for him in its regular classes, and everyone in the church stands to gain from this endeavor to meet the need of its weakest member.

Teachers expecting to have educable pupils in their classes should be prepared in these ways:

1. They must love and accept these pupils for what they are, realizing that they are incapable of attaining the intellectual levels of normal students but that they do want and need a chance to display their limited ability. Teachers must never be upset or angered with the retardate's lack of knowledge, for he already keenly feels his insufficiencies.[6]

2. The teacher should be prepared to accept the retardate's human shortcoming, and try to understand his deficiencies by reading or enrolling in introductory (college) courses on exceptional children.[7]

During class sessions, the teacher can help his student in these ways:

1. Never ask him to do anything which he knows is beyond his ability, such as reading, writing on paper or the board, singing songs alone. Some feel that even the placing of a Bible in front of a retardate is probably the wrong thing to do, for he can become upset simply by thinking that fellow students expect him to be able to read.

2. Do have him perform tasks which you know he will be able to accomplish with complete success, and in which he can "show off" to his classmates. He can pass out hymnals and other material, usher and take the collection, hold up and handle visual aids for the teacher, post material on bulletin

boards, and perhaps even be a greeter in his own department.

3. A teacher should encourage this student to participate by answering questions for which he volunteers. In the instance where a teacher gets an inexact answer, he should try to make it fit in some way so that he does not completely deflate the pupil's ego. This is especially important for the student who is rarely verbal. Conversely, the annoyingly loud and verbal retardate may need the teacher's strong hand of discipline, for he must not be allowed to disturb the smooth flow of class interaction.

Some churches begin ministering to retardates because these children belong to families within the congregation. Jimmy was one such student. His parents had joined the small, suburban church long before he was born, and they enrolled him in the preschool department as a matter of course. If people noticed that he seemed to be in constant motion,§ that he acted erratically and with strikingly babyish mannerisms, no one really wanted to point out that he had a deficiency. His parents began to be apologetic, saying that he had a speech problem; however, he continued being an acceptable pupil in the preschool department. His mother taught there, and was able to exert disciplinary action whenever he began disturbing the general activity.

At five years of age Jimmy went to school, and there he joined a class for children who were able to attain a limited education. Jimmy needed this new learning experience, which would be specially structured to aid him in reaching the outer limits of his ability. However, his parents felt an emotional devastation. They had never before admitted — even to themselves — the extent of their son's handicap. Now many questions privately plagued them. Was the acceptance which their family experienced in the church and community only

---

§ Hyperactivity: More than the normal amount of action; frequent display of change of moods, with the accompanying inability to concentrate on a given task. The hyperactive retardate is dangerous to other persons only if he has never been disciplined not to be aggressive toward others.

superficial? Would their pastor and Christian friends turn away and be repulsed by the facts of mental retardation? In other words, would the spiritual and social security of their family unit be endangered? Would it dissolve?

However, the Christian education staff had already begun planning a place in the Sunday school so that Jimmy could go along with his age group in the regular classes. Special planning for him involved the conditioning of his teachers to cope with his deficiencies.

Thus Jimmy's parents felt secure within the church family because the church worked to meet his needs. At the first-grade level Jimmy gained an unquestioned place in his own age group. Baumeister claims that if an EMH child does experience social rejection, it is due to unacceptable behavior patterns rather than low academic ability.[8]

As Jimmy grew older, he also grew farther away from the interest levels of his peers, due to his inability to match their intellectual pace. He may grow to be alone in later teen years (when normal youngsters begin leaving home for school and work) unless he develops a close friendship with someone in the church or community whose ability is more like his own.

THE SPECIAL CLASS

Trainable mentally retarded students must be given a class and teacher (or teachers) of their own.‖ Grouping of a large number of TMRs would probably have to follow the suggestions given by Stubblefield, in other words, chronological age, plus physical, mental, social and emotional needs. Those retardates unable to hear or speak would be grouped alone because different teaching methods would have to be used with them, methods first designed to establish communication between teacher and student.

However, Cruickshank reiterates one teaching principle

‖ See chap. 2 for characteristics of TMR persons.

which needs to be applied to all types of student groups: the teacher must establish his authority as leader of the class, whose members realize that he expects them to work together as a unit.[9] He must guide his group; this is the best criteria for accepting trainables in the Sunday school class. Teachers should decide whether or not the behavior patterns of a prospective student will allow him to join a group without disrupting its activity, remembering that Sunday school is not the place for the maladjusted retarded child to learn the basics of social grace. Parents should begin this training at home.

The visitor to a Sunday school classroom for TMRs in a large northern city immediately spotted the trouble which eventually caused the Christian education board of the church to disband the class. Though the ratio of teachers to pupils was one to one, chaos reigned because the teachers could not work with the students' hyperactive tendencies and control the class.

On the other hand, Margaret Hudson offers this encouragement to the school which can provide one teacher for every trainable retardate: some brain-damaged children cannot adapt to a classroom situation until they have had a period of adjustment and an opportunity to acquire learning skills on a one-to-one basis. Due to a mixture of types of brain damage, environmental factors, and the problem of supervision (not enough teachers and assistants), it is not always possible to handle a hyperactive child in the classroom. Yet they can learn if they are protected from the massed stimuli in a group situation.[10]

Cruickshank further explains the trainable child's need of the one-to-one teaching experience: "He must strengthen his self-image, his sense of personal worth. Until he is comfortable with himself, he will not succeed in peer relationships. As he grows in his own eyes, he will be more ready to move into group activity."[11] Teachers may slowly increase group activity but should keep it within the child's tolerance level.[12]

In light of the foregoing information, a church should not place the class for trainable students in the same room with another department. Besides triggering hyperactivity in the retarded students, other kinds of problems would arise. For example, the retarded would wander around and possibly disrupt other classes. Noise is also a factor complicated by the need to frequently change activity in the special class. Teachers must encourage retarded pupils to be verbally expressive, and pupils often do so in loud and erratic sounds, from which other classes should be protected.

BUILDINGS AND EQUIPMENT

The well-planned environment contributes immeasurably to the overall welfare of this student, who is capable of being as well adjusted as the normal child. However, churches must make greater and more thoughtful room provision for him than for nonhandicapped children. Some of the previously implied specifications for a desirable special education room are these:

1. Minimal standards set by the city and insurance companies of health, heat and fire prevention, plus consideration of the needs of physically handicapped pupils[13] such as location and accessibility.[14]

2. Location in a desirable part of the building where any other teacher would be glad to hold class, perhaps in a quiet spot and away from other classes.[15]

3. The room needs a ventilating system which supplies clean air (without drafts) in adequate quantity to eliminate odors.♯[16]

4. An environment which stimulates the healthy student is inappropriate for the retarded, especially those who suffer

---

♯ This point cannot be given enough stress. One of the most severe problems faced by the authors in their classroom concerned odors. Some mentally retarded are not conscious of body needs and are prone to neglect certain necessary body functions, causing strong odors, especially in females. With this in mind, it is imperative that the classroom be adequately ventilated.

hyperactivity, for they cannot refrain from reacting to un-essential stimuli in the classroom.[17]

Most of the complexities of the retarded child's learning disabilities cannot be altered,[18] so there remains only the solution of creating an educational environment which will face him with a minimum of distractions. This environment is just the opposite of that which we conceive for the normal student — bright, stimulating colors with many centers of interest to capture and ignite his imagination. Comfort might be the only similarity between the ideal learning situation for the retarded and normal student, and even that aspect must be worked out in differing physical arrangements.

Those charged with planning facilities to house a class for trainable mentally retarded students might follow some of these guidelines set down by Cruickshank for distractible pupils: match the colors of floor, furniture, woodwork and walls; provide one bulletin board and post only pictures there; shut off communication systems (which may have been installed in more modern churches); remove all furniture which is not absolutely essential to teaching activity. This advice may seem stark, at the very least. But this kind of environment is actually designed to shield the student from all possible stimuli outside of the learning opportunity being given him by the teacher.[19] He must be careful to dress in muted colors, for bright colors only excite the student and draw his attention away from almost everything which the teacher is trying to do with him or with a group.

5. Tables and chairs should be adjusted to the proper height of the individual so that sitting posture is healthful and comfortable. Classrooms, if they are organized according to developmental levels rather than the chronological age level, should have chairs of different sizes. These persons grow at a slower rate and appear to the observer to be an assorted arrangement of sizes and shapes. Individual needs must be catered to in the classroom to produce the desired learning.

It is important, therefore, that the Christian teacher understand the individual needs and differences of his mentally handicapped group. Formica table-tops will help in clean-up operations.

A piano is helpful, especially in the classes for retarded youth and adults. The following should be accessible in the church school: records, rhythm instruments, toys, books, and other supplies as necessary to reach the goals for the trainable retarded in the Sunday school.

SUMMARY

The church which elects to minister to the mentally retarded has as its first duty the proper placement of the students. Educators differentiate between the educable and the trainable retarded. The educable mentally retarded, whose IQ rises high enough for a limited education, should go along with his own age in the regular classes of the Sunday school. Trainable retarded pupils should never be placed in regular classes because their total needs are far too demanding for successful integration with normal students.

Neither will teachers be successful in handling these children in the classroom which has been outfitted for the normal, healthy child. The Christian education board and trustees should work together in planning an environmentally congenial classroom for trainable pupils who display highly intensified emotional, social and physical reactions to the people and things surrounding them. Since these reactions continually interfere with their attempts to learn, much of the success of the teaching attempts depends upon the extent to which the room has been planned exclusively for their comfort. A new room in a new building presents possibilities of creating the ideal atmosphere, but churches also can adapt space in older buildings for the special class.

6

Who Shall Teach the Mentally Retarded?

SUNDAY, 9:30 A.M. Mrs. Bracken, special education teacher for the Sunday school class for the trainable mentally retarded of the Midtown Community Church, stands greeting her seven primary-age pupils. She extends her sincere greeting and reinforces her words with some type of personal, individualized attention to each child.

Seven-year-old John bubbles with the news that his favorite baseball team won their game yesterday. Mrs. Bracken replies that she hopes his team will win again today. "Yes, they're playing a home game," says John, "and I'm going to watch it." Mrs. Bracken knows how important this sports interest is to the mentally retarded youngster, and she is careful to indicate often that baseball is a good thing for John to follow and enjoy.

"Help me, help me!" Anne yells as she stands waiting for someone to remove her coat. At home someone always does every task for Anne, so she expects Mrs. Bracken to jump to her call in just the way her family responds. Instead, the teacher stands nearby with encouraging words and gestures to help the child remove her own coat which, in fact, she can do. Although some of the others cannot, Mrs. Bracken encourages them to learn. She puts Billy's fingers around a button and helps him push it through the hole and then guides him to the spot where he can hang his coat on a hook and shows him

60

how. She supports each child in the learning experiences which she has planned for him.

The teacher sets the tone, pace, and mood of everything that takes place in the classroom. Retarded pupils will respond to teaching efforts after she encourages each one, thus she must appeal to each in the way which is most meaningful to him. She sets the stage through warmth and friendliness for the moment when she will call the class to order. They respond to her authority because she has proved to be their friend, and they experience in her authority a security and comfort. Mrs. Bracken has the ability to make her class feel like worthwhile individuals and, as a result, the retarded want to behave to please her.

The success of a church school program for the mentally retarded comes in direct proportion to the ability of its teacher. Certain competencies — spiritual, emotional and academic — are necessary if his work with the trainable retarded proves effective. As a priority, the special education teacher must be a Christian if he is to accomplish spiritual results in the lives of his pupils. He must have genuine Christian character, whose facets include patience, respect for and sensibility to the human need, "and an appreciation of the inherent worth of every human being."[1] Christ Himself set the example of dealing with human weakness — never turning away from the needy, always helping with a word, a touch, or a transformation, and preserving human dignity. These same qualities must not be lacking in the teacher of the retarded.

Christian character and professional background should go hand in hand in the choice of leadership for the church's special education classes, and the Christian education board must place the spiritual welfare of the mentally handicapped at the top of its list of goals for the class. That welfare demands that a teacher have a clear picture of his task, with a good working knowledge of mental deficiency, or at least a familiarity with learning disorders. No one will ever be effective with the retarded unless he works from a basic knowledge of learning problems. "He needs to know how theory, general procedure and specific tasks can be effectively combined in a program which helps each child learn in accord with his own potential."[2] Never does a person teach the retarded as a group, for each child or youth manifests his learning problems a little differently within the large framework of disorders.

Another goal for the teacher is that of stimulating pupils to their highest level of performance, which by average standards is low indeed. Thus no untrained teacher will be capable of providing the many activities, wide variety of materials, shortened sessions and adequate stimulation[3] — all of which are necessary ingredients in either the public school or the church school program for the mentally retarded.

Also, the professionally competent teacher within the church's special education program more easily detaches himself from pitying the children's liability and, rather, directs his compassion into giving them positive and specific opportunities to learn, to feel self-accomplished. The untrained teacher often uses his own feelings to replace knowledge, something which happens with many teacher aides who tend to want to do everything *for* the children. Their motives are beyond question, but they lack objectivity toward retardation because they must help the pupils learn to do for themselves. Because such objectivity becomes an innate thing for those who have had training in the theory and methods of helping the trainable retarded, Christian educators who work with the retarded feel that any church which undertakes special education without the appropriate personnel will miserably fail. One recommendation for building an adequate staff is: "The minimum training program should include consultation with professional people (both in retardation and Christian education), supervised contact with the retarded, and the reading of basic books on retardation."[4]

The test of special ability with the retarded has not ended

when a teacher finishes a training course about mental retardation. In reality, it may only begin there. The mentally handicapped continually confront the teacher with a need to review his own personality traits and the depths of his maturity, for he deals successfully with his pupils commensurate with the way he balances his feelings toward them. The following checklist of attitudes is one to which every teacher and worker with the retarded should give frequent and prayerful attention:[5]

1. *Am I comfortable with this person?* No one can honestly give quick affirmation to this question unless he has had sufficient experience with the retarded to know that as a group they have some social problems which often prove offensive. One public-school teacher who volunteered as an aide in the special class of the Sunday school of her church, recalls the shock of her first experiences in that class: "Many of the children had runny noses, and it nearly sickened me to have to wipe their faces clean. But I survived that test, and wiping noses became routine. The children — their needs and personalities — seemed to outweigh all of the annoying little things." In fact, the person who does become genuinely comfortable with the retardate remolds himself to the needs of that person. His own self-image takes second place, and he says in effect by his actions and attitudes, "I'm here for you, and I'll be whatever you need me to be in order that you may use your energy positively." That's what we call "being at ease" with the retardate, and he will be able to feel it.

Conversely, the person who holds an ideal image of human beings will be unable to work effectively with the retarded, either as a teacher or an aide. Nor should he try, because he is emotionally unable to accept human imperfection.

Those in special education become attached to the retarded both because of and in spite of their imperfection. Also, friendship with them develops perhaps in the reverse order of that which happens among more healthy people. We are normally attracted to a person through his apparent perfection of those character traits for which we look in a new friend. Liking what we see on the surface, we go about cultivating the friendship. And it is during that cultivation that we discover the cracks and crevices which are not visible on the surface. But in the case of the retarded, only as parents, teachers and others live and work with them, do they see the good and strong and positive characteristics. One man who has become an authority in the field describes his own beginning experience with the retarded: "Before observing these children, I thought I would be unable to work with them because of their disfigured and uncoordinated condition. Now they seem almost normal in appearance, and I am fully aware of their need to learn."[6]

The ideal teacher is relatively free of the fear which would prohibit him from being relaxed with the retardate, who tends to respond in like manner to a calm, purposeful teacher. The severely retarded becomes violent when he feels insecure with his surroundings, and the level of maturity within his teacher often determines how well the child can learn to deal with his tendency toward tantrums. The teacher first tries to provide the pupil with nonfrustrating learning experiences, then he deals authoritatively with his angry outbursts. In one such classroom scene, a tall, powerful retardate actually became sheepish in the face of receiving a severe reprimand from his teacher, who was perhaps half his size and weight. Teachers must first prove themselves to be completely trustworthy, providing pupils with an unusual amount of support on a continual, dependable basis. Then when the teacher stands up and is strong and authoritative, the pupil has an exemplary emotional basis from which to grow.

2. *What are my feelings toward him?* Do they change? A person can feel perfectly comfortable with the retarded, and yet never experience a change of attitude about them. That is, some people have fixed in their minds that the retarded are a

static phenomenon, a group of individuals who never grow or change. Thus they feel justified in looking at them as nothing more than symbols of human inability. Teachers and other workers who come with this attitude and still have a desire to serve the mentally retarded, soon change their minds about the human potential in these pupils. For a retarded child or youth is flesh and blood, mind and emotions, a person who knows very well whether or not his teacher warms up to him as the (Sunday school) days go by. He knows when he begins to tailor learning situations to fit his needs. He can feel when the teacher's feelings are changing, when the teacher is getting to know and appreciate him for himself. A teacher's smile of recognition, his praise of work, all tell the pupil just how his teacher feels about him.

3. *Can I accept the pupil where he is and not show irritation at his efforts to learn?* Every retarded child is unique in that he fits into no uniform place of human development, either physically or intellectually. The teacher needs patience,[7] first to find the learning level of each pupil, and then to be willing to wait long periods to actually see definite changes.[8] He cannot set standards for his pupils which conform to his own ideas of success because (1) the pupil will never fully absorb the sophisticated religious and economic value system of people with a normal mentality, and (2) he is both mentally and physically unable to perform the mechanics of learning experiences at the same rate as a normal child. Thus the teacher must (1) be very aware of just what learning experiences the pupil is ready for, then (2) extend his support and patience to the learning efforts being made by the youngster, (3) remain calm and unruffled when he fails, and also (4) be able to sense when he is ready to learn something new.

The teacher who does combine patience with a sensitivity to the needs of each student best succeeds at his job. For example, consider a group of primary-age retardates trying to

illustrate something in that day's lesson. The teacher accepts
the children where they are, which means that many of them
do not have enough muscle development to hold a crayon.*
Normal primary-age children color, draw, and cut out pictures.
The method can become a good one for use with retarded
children, provided teachers are prepared to actually go
through the motions of doing these things with pupils by
guiding their fingers and giving them verbal encouragement.
The teacher asks pupils to draw a simple object at first, and
then gives simple directions, "Let's draw a picture of the ball
which the little girl was holding as she sat on Jesus' lap."

Some pupils will do very well; others will do nothing.
Yet the teacher must show equal pleasure with whatever attempts they do make, for the retardate will learn little or nothing when he can sense a spirit of irritation from his teacher.
Thus the teacher fails in his goals if ever he betrays disappointment or dissatisfaction with a pupil's performance, and
in a very real way, the irritable, misunderstanding Sunday
school teacher does little to build the retardate's concept of
his loving heavenly Father. Sunday school should, after all,
be the place where this child receives compassionate aid for
his most basic needs. One of these means to be accepted by
the people in his world. Of this, Baumeister says, "If pupils
experience sufficient interaction with adults, they gradually
become able to achieve independently and without the constant need for approval. Those not receiving sufficient adult
approval during school days will always remain more needful
of overt acceptance."[9]

4. *Am I rigid in my approach?* No retarded youngster is
able to respond to an unbending, unaccommodating attitude
from his teacher. He must never approach a child with the
vocal or implied intention, "This is what I'm going to teach
you, and this is the way you are going to learn it."

Jean Saunders, special education teacher for the retarded

---

* See chap. 2 on TMR characteristics and chap. 7 on teaching methods.

in the New York public school system, illustrates how this approach can frustrate and immobilize the retarded in learning experiences. Speaking to a group of students and teachers of retarded children, she asks them to imagine that she had come to give them a crash course in computer programming. First she informs them that by the end of her lecture and demonstration they will, in fact, have absorbed the know-how to be programmers. Then she proceeds to lecture, demonstrating programming techniques, and subsequently leaving the room. She tells the group that the sheaf of information piled atop her desk should be programmed in her absence, and that she will return in half an hour to see how well her instructions have been carried out.

What would be the mood of that group of people if such a thing really happened to them? They would probably feel frustration, resentment and despair because this teacher evidently didn't care that few if any of them would be capable of doing computer programming after only one lesson. She just said in effect, "This is what I'm going to teach you, and you'd better learn it." Mrs. Saunders points out through this illustration that everyone has some kind of learning handicap; everyone is incapable of learning or of doing something. And the rigid "do it or else" approach with the mentally retarded child is the quickest way to drive him back into his shell of familiar frustration.

The teacher who uses flexible methods and expectations has at least begun to set up the ideal learning situation for these pupils. Daily schedules must have variety and a constant change of tempo, for teachers and parents can be precise in neither the rate at which a retardate learns nor in the media or method through which he finally catches on to something. All goals are long-range; pupils reach them slowly.

For example, the use of music has proven to be very effective with retarded pupils, so Sunday school teachers can apply it liberally in reinforcing lessons and as a simple tool of

instilling joy. But suppose that in teaching a song, the instructor notices that one little boy, Henry, substitutes a word here
and there in place of the proper verse. Should she correct him
for the sake of a mistaken word? Probably not. She can question to discover if the substituted words have the meaning
for him which the song intends, and she may suggest that he
insert the proper word. But never should Henry be pressured
to sing the right words which might cost him the loss of the
meaning of the song. It matters little that he is always proper
about one or two words. What matters more is that he experiences a certain kind of fulfillment through singing, and that
he knows he is worshiping God in song.†

5. *Am I satisfied with him?* The very honest teacher will
put it this way: "Does the quantity and quality of his learning
growth show that I am doing my job fully?" The teacher can
answer affirmatively and thus be satisfied with pupil progress
when he has given extra effort to compensate for pupil-learn-
ing deficits.

However, parents frequently show dissatisfaction with the
progress of their retarded child, sometimes literally begging a
teacher for evidence that their child is making great strides,
and they are puzzled when teachers seem pleased with only a
little progress. Anxiety wells up within parents when the retardate brings home schoolwork and displays it beside that
done by his normal brothers and sisters. It rarely compares
well, and perhaps the family uses this occasion to pick on the
handicapped child. Everyone is hurt because he once again
has failed to meet a standard and to gain stature in parental
eyes. The child's ego is shattered, and his parents feel as
though they have been dealt yet another disappointing blow.[10]

When parents come to school asking why a son or daughter has not progressed in the very simplest of things, the teach-

---

† Christian educators do strongly suggest that songs used in worship be
those which the retarded can understand. Otherwise, much of the Sunday
school's teaching purpose is lost.

er must first be patient with these frustrated parents. Then he must demonstrate that he is pleased with the child's work, that he *is* progressing, and *how* he is progressing. The child's work will be too imperfect for the norm of children his age, but he cannot judge this for himself. Rather, his family should consider his lesser accomplishments to be signs that he has begun to learn, and not that he has arrived.[11] Building the retardate's ego as well as his ability has been the teaching goal, not that he should measure up to other children in the family.

6. *Can I set limits, then relax and allow this person to grow?* Setting limits entails two things: establishing clear behavioral bounds, and determining the goal for a given learning experience.

Every trainable can learn obedience regarding the things he can and cannot do in th eclsasroom. He needs continual reinforcing against forbidden behavior, whether it be creating class disturbances through tantrums or by use of other attention-getting techniques. The teacher must be physically strong, firm and kind in order to gain control of his class, or they will control him — and the idealistically conceived Sunday school class will quickly be reduced to a baby-sitting session. The teacher sometimes finds it necessary to bodily move an unwilling child, or actually make him do something. Perhaps the teacher helps the child comply with a command by assisting him. For example, after saying, "Sit down," he places the child in his seat.

Setting limits also means that a teacher sets up a frame within which the child tests his ability. This frame consists in part of the teacher's own personality, for the dependable, consistent teacher becomes a foundation for the pupil, a structure against which he can push and pull in his struggle to grow and learn.

But primarily, the "structured"[12] learning situation refers to certain tasks which are successfully completed through a

predetermined and precise set of instructions. Learning instructions must always have bounds, or the mentally retarded
child will constantly divert himself, get lost and never reach
a goal. For example, there is the child who wants to begin the
class "good morning" song before removing his coat. He is
proceeding unacceptably, but perhaps he has not had sufficient
reminding that everyone takes off his coat before class begins.
The little boy has simply patterned his own behavior before
the teachers had opportunity to show him a better way. The
teacher needs to plan, then demonstrate, and then demonstrate
again; he does not restructure behavior in a day. Children
will form their own approach to all of the numerous activities
which go on in a Sunday school hour. Many of them will start
out wrong and become frustrated unless teachers are quick to
form a routine for each retardate, see that he can carry out
instructions, and then that he actually does so. It is at this
point that mentally retarded pupils can actually begin learning. Teachers may relax and trust the pupil's initiative after
they have planned a goal which he can actually reach, shown
him how to do it over and over again, disciplined his attempts
by helping him not to divert or misbehave, and, finally, provided an overabundant amount of praise when the pupil
succeeded.

This concept of patterned, structured behavior for the retarded child is strange to some parents and teachers. As a
result, the Sunday school may have to cope with the undisciplined retardate because parents have tried to compensate for
the terrible extent of the child's handicap by being permissive.
However, such permissiveness only acts to inhibit the child's
total growth, and it can never be the compensating power
which the parents intended. Teachers of the retarded, like
parents, must reach the point in their own emotional health
where they will strive with the pupil toward good behavior
and toward positive learning patterns.

7. *Have I discussed his shortcomings in front of him?*

This question suggests that the teacher's personal integrity plays a part in the success of his classroom efforts. It does. The teacher's total character can have a negative effect upon pupils if they detect any unsympathetic or unspiritual quality in him. In fact, pupils pick out negative qualities much more quickly than can be imagined, and sometimes they pinpoint character defects which a person has not seen within himself. Normally, these things are rationalized away by calling them human weaknesses, excusable failings. More often perhaps, we should offer these things "to God as sins to be forgiven."[13]

The teacher needs to develop sensitivity for the retardate's feelings at all times and in all company, particularly when he is present to overhear the things which are said about him. Someone may unintentionally belittle a child or youth with remarks about his inability in public conversation. The retarded may have reason to doubt his teacher if he overhears an objective analysis of his learning rate. Then he might begin reacting to his resulting feelings of inadequacy by withdrawing, being aggressive, showing frustration, dislike or indifference in class.[14] Perhaps the teacher praises his work each day but fails to mention these things during the parent-teacher conferences. All of these things work to tell the retardate that his teacher has much less confidence in him than he claims.

The teacher divests his pupil of yet another security when he fails to build him up both in public and in private. The retarded pupil already has constant reminders of his inadequacy, except in the confines of the special classroom. He may be the same age and size as his normal friends but unable to join in sports and games at their level due to his poor coordination and thinking power. And even his family may demand that he act like a normal child.[15] Thus he sorely needs the confidence that his teacher will not degrade him.

8. *Can I help my fellow church members understand retardation and the need to extend social acceptance to the mentally retarded?* A teacher's own character, his standing in

the church and professional community, and his enthusiastic spirit toward his work will largely determine how well a church accepts and adjusts to the class for the trainable retarded.

It is probably a well-known fact that deviation in human appearance or behavior tends to foster fear and misunderstanding. Retardation is an all-too-obvious human deviation which can destroy a comfortable, relaxed atmosphere. Young couples begin wondering if retardation will strike their unborn child. Everyone hesitates in conversation with these youngsters; in fact, people avoid talking to them. They look different — a trait which in itself is offensive and threatening to some. The special education teacher therefore acts as a liaison between his class members and that segment of the church which needs to grow in understanding and acceptance of retarded members.

No Sunday school teacher will be able to succeed without emotional involvement with his retarded student. Love is of prime importance — love for this student who is different. The teacher will only be able to achieve something with the student when his therapy is love, which must be given to the child each session. Many retarded students will respond only for persons they love. Through the love of the teacher the child can feel the love of God.[16]

TEACHER AIDES

Who is the teacher aide? As the term suggests, this person comes as a helper. Aides can be parents of the retarded or people out of the congregation who want to do something in and for the special class. However, aides are not usually qualified teachers, simply because there are rarely more than one or two special education professionals, even in a very large church. Nonetheless, the untrained person often has many fine qualities which can be used effectively with handicapped children.

The best teacher aide has a submissive spirit on two counts. First, he looks to the teacher to decide what will be his class responsibilities. Second, he abandons his own methods of operation and efficiency when he is helping a pupil to learn how to do something.

Teacher aides are a necessary addition to a classroom for trainables because each child needs a great deal of personal attention, and there is a continual flow of housekeeping chores which need caring for *now* so that class activity can proceed amid order. Thus the person who comes "to help the retarded" may feel disappointed in having to play the mother — baby-sitter role. The teacher aide in the special class will fail unless he initially bases his Christian service on the intent of being "all things to all men," for an aide is needed to perform simple service tasks for the children and to restore order after painting sessions or refreshment time.[17]

Volunteers in the class for trainables must discard their own notions about teaching and alter their expectations of pupil performance. It is one thing to be efficient in keeping the classroom tidy, but it is quite another to be rigid and demand perfection in the children. Since they are not capable of doing anything which would meet normal adult standards, the aide must bow to the trainable children's need by never insisting that they do things his way. If the child seems to be growing through a divergent method, then the teacher aide must strain his own thinking and try to conceive the steps of the child's logic.

Some retarded youngsters are immediately lovable, while others become objects of teacher-love by the very depth of their need for human support and acceptance. However, aides are to exercise an objective love and never *do* everything for the trainable, because the pupil needs help in learning to do for himself. Aides must be willing to stand by and allow the child to struggle with a task, lend a helping hand in demonstration, and see that his struggle does not lead to frustration and tantrums. An aide may learn these techniques slowly, but once they become second nature to him, he will be invaluable as an assistant to the teacher. This can also be the proof-test of whether or not a young person has potential as a special education teacher. This type of supervised practice into which a teacher aide can turn his voluntary job is the only way of determining whether he has insight into the retardate's limitations and abilities, can relate to them, and thus create activities and programs suitable to the growth and development of retarded children.[18]

The teacher aide lends these definite advantages to classroom activity:[19]

1. Teachers can plan more activity, and use increased and diverse materials. Aides put plans into action by taking time to help each child. A lone teacher would not have time to see that every child carried through on a project. He would have to plan simpler and less demanding projects, and fewer pupils would get individualized attention.

2. The teacher himself can give more attention to each child when there is another person present in the room to help maintain order. Parents have noted that the retarded child develops all-round better response when he receives abundant attention in class.

3. The aide can help a new pupil to more quickly integrate into classroom activity. The aide strives for early identification with the new child so that he can provide the moral support which the pupil needs in adjusting to this new situation.

4. Finally, the aide should increase the effectiveness of a limited professional staff. That is, one teacher may have to be responsible for more than a handful of trainables. Many teacher aides can absorb teaching methods and goals and apply them as they work with the children.

SUMMARY

The qualified teacher is the key to the success of a Sunday school class for the trainable mentally retarded. He must have an established faith in Jesus Christ as Saviour and Provider of eternal life. He needs the assets of an outgoing personality and training in both Christian education and education for the mentally retarded.

His maturity and flexibility will be tested week after week in the classroom. His success with the retarded will depend upon how well he is unselfishly and objectively answering the following questions:

Am I comfortable with mentally retarded persons?

What are my feelings toward the pupil? Do they change?

Can I accept him where he is and not show irritation at his efforts to learn?

Am I rigid in my approach?

Am I satisfied with the pupil?

Can I set limits, then relax and allow this person to grow?

Have I discussed his shortcomings in front of him?

Can I help my fellow church members understand retardation and the need to extend social acceptance to the mentally retarded?

The teacher aide comes to the class for trainables as a helper, and not in a teacher role. His duties are the housekeeping chores which may be necessary during class, and he also sits with the children to strengthen discipline and to help them participate in each activity.

7

What Teaching Methods Should Be Used?

"A TEACHING PROCEDURE is a course of action followed for the purpose of helping a person achieve certain learning."[1] Since the purpose of teaching is to effect some change in future situations,[2] a teaching method is a good procedure only if it helps the person achieve the desired growth and learning. In order to achieve this growth, a variety of methods must be employed when teaching the mentally retarded because no one method will be successful with all cases. One individual learns by one method; another will succeed better with a different method.[3]

How does the teacher teach the trainable child? Marie Egg says, "As far as humanly possible, treat the retarded child like a normal child, but do not expect him to react like one."[4] One visitor stood aghast as the Sunday school teacher asked her retarded pupils, "Did you ever think why Jesus healed the blind man?" Of course the teacher realized that the students have probably not thought about it, but she treated them as healthy children, not expecting them to respond in the same manner as normal children.

The retarded child, unlike the healthy student, cannot recognize relationships or make connections; neither can he draw analogies. The teacher, therefore, cannot be content to use Sunday school curriculum prepared for the normal child with his trainable students, for the material needs to be adapted to their needs and lesson plans must be made which will allow them to respond to the stimuli provided in the Sunday school. To teach them Christian concepts, one must begin, as it were, at the beginning. Because the teacher needs to make sure that each concept is carefully preserved, practice is absolutely necessary. Repetition is essential and can take various forms, such as games and role-play. Such play activity, properly used, helps the child practice the knowledge he has gained and prepares him for new learning experiences.

Coupled with the necessary longer learning period for mentally retarded pupils is the imperative need to individualize instruction and technique for them. Good planning must include motivation for the learner and also repetition or drill. Experiences should be provided that are relevant to the pupils' experience.

Various techniques have proved successful in primary research with trainable students. The teacher wishing to utilize these techniques for maximum pupil benefit should keep two factors in mind: (1) Stress the practical and tangible.[5] For example, a Bible study which includes a culture and customs not understood by the retarded, or abstract symbols that are completely beyond them, must be reduced to terms with which the pupils can identify. (2) Capitalize on individual mental and manual ability.[6] In other words, be sure to increase the motivations for a more able student.

STORYTELLING

"Tell it again! Tell it again!" Trainable mentally retarded pupils love stories because they kindle their meager imagination. They also influence their conduct, so much so that the teacher is able to better lead the person in learning experiences. However, a story should not be used for entertainment value; it should be used only when it helps achieve a learning purpose.[7]

Whatever the teacher tells the trainable pupil, he accepts as true; therefore he accepts fairy tales just as he does Bible stories, for he can make no distinction between the real and the unreal, between fact and fancy, or between Cinderella and David and the giant. This places a great responsibility upon the teacher, for the content of his belief is imparted to his student. Retarded persons are not expected to grasp the intricate truths as found in the Scriptures, but neither are they to be denied the road to salvation. Teaching needs to consider their needs, abilities and capabilities.

Teacher preparation may include these steps:

> Read the story several times, visualizing each character and incident.
> Note descriptive words which you may want to use.
> Know how you will begin the story.
> Note the various steps in development.
> Know how you will end the story.
> Tell the story aloud. Retell it several times if necessary, until it becomes so much a part of you that it will seem you are relating something you experienced personally.[8]

A good method of testing storytelling ability is for the teacher to listen as though he were in the shoes of his retarded students to a story which he has tape-recorded. He will easily discover errors and weaknesses of presentation.

Ethel Barrett gives general points on delivery suitable for use with the trainable retarded pupil:

> You must be a good salesman.
> Be sincere — the real thing.
> Earnestness is essential.
> Wholeheartedness.
> Enthusiasm.
> Be yourself.[9]

Stories of relevance to the normal child will be of little interest to the trainable mentally retarded. Even as many stories geared to the age level of the normal person would be inappropriate for the adolescent, the teacher should create stories geared to the needs of the person with whom he is dealing, taking into consideration both the mental and the chronological age.

The teacher should use sensory words to help overcome vocabulary limitations of students. Rhythm and repetition are both necessary and delightful to the retarded. Short, simple sentences are used effectively, but care must be exercised not to "deflate" his chronological age.

Characters seem to come alive when conversation is used in the story, so the teacher should use dialogue, starting out with two persons and creating a conversation between them. He should practice and practice until he is able to effectively reflect the voices. Sack puppets, one on each hand, may move their mouths to create the visual image of conversation.

The trainable mentally retarded cannot understand all Bible stories, for something in the story must be related to his past experiences. Since he is very literal, stories dealing with abstractions will not be understood. Here again, caution must be exercised in choosing Bible stories pertaining to the interests of the pupil's chronological age. Choose stories with a positive lesson and avoid those that would threaten his security. If the Bible story is based on some area of his understanding it may then become the basis for religious teaching.

Various methods of storytelling should be used. The spoken word alone leaves a clouded, temporary impression on the retarded, so flannelgraph is an excellent visual aid. The creation, for example, can unfold before their very eyes as they see the sun, moon, and stars. Lap flannelboards can be made for each child, so he can actually tell the story with the teacher. Take a small sturdy box with hinged lid and cover with contact paper. Cover the lid with flannel material and use it for a lap flannelboard in the classroom. Figures can be kept inside the box. Flash cards are also helpful if the pictures chosen are readily understood in the context of the pupil's experiences.

A combination of methods can be used for effective story-telling. As the story of creation unfolds via flannelgraph, it can be reinforced with tape-recorder or record-player narration and sound effects. As Adam named the animals, play different animal sounds. Such records can often be purchased in the Christian bookstore, or the teacher can make his own recording during a trip to the zoo or farm. Another way to make stories come alive is to use a split-35 mm. Stori-strip projector,* or a Show 'n Tell.† As the record plays, the full-color scenes change on the screen at exactly the right moment. Teachers can also make a story wheel and use it effectively. Cut two large circles from poster board. Around the outer edge of one, paste small Bible story pictures. From the other, cut a wedge large enough to reveal one picture at a time. With a brad put the two circles together.

Too much questioning of children should be avoided; therefore, the class should summarize the story as a group. Children who are unable to read or write should draw an object from the story, perhaps one small detail within their capability.

CREATIVE PLAY-ACTING

Children love play-acting, an instinct which is an integral part of the equipment of the early years. Through make-believe, the child strives for the feel of the new world unfolding about him. With real fervor he nurses his teddy bear, and imitates his trip to the market, including the noise of the fire engine that he saw across the street. When creative play-acting is included in an activity program, this natural instinct is made to serve educational purposes. This is not true of the trainable mentally retarded, however; they need to be taught how to use their imaginations, and they need constant encouragement to do so. Their interest in surroundings is slight.[10]

---

* Can be purchased from Gospel Light Publications, Glendale, California.

† This is produced by General Electric and can be purchased from David C. Cook Publishing Company, Elgin, Illinois.

The Sunday school teacher for the trainable mentally retarded faces a situation that calls for unique adjustments. His basic purpose is to help the person to understand and know God in such a way that His redeeming love is evidenced in his life.‡ Drama can be a way of achieving these aims. To help the retarded become "more mature," he must help them live free from the chains of self-pity and self-hate, accepting themselves as they are, and thereby accepting others. Time devoted to drama in the church school program can be richly rewarding with these persons. The material presented should follow the theme contained in the curriculum. Much careful research is needed in so complex a field if the greatest benefits are to accrue from the hours devoted to this study.

PANTOMIME

Recreating in pantomime the simple and familiar activities of the mentally retarded is recommended as the best method of beginning a drama project. The word *pantomime* means "the expression or communication of an idea through action alone, without the assistance of the spoken word."[11] This type of play-acting may be performed on many levels; for example, the church school teacher can use pantomime in acting out ideas from the lesson; ways to help in the home, school, etc.; and in scores of imaginative situations. However, with the retarded, the simplest form must be utilized.

It is important for the teacher to create in the retarded a "mind picture" of the situation, and also to interest them in a total situation or story, not merely the activity itself. It must be a purposeful activity if it is to meet the needs of the individual.§

---

‡ Chap. 5 portrays more vividly the religious consciousness of the mentally retarded, thus enabling the reader to assess what the goals should be for religious education for the retarded.

§ The authors have had experience with the use of pantomime in teaching the trainable mentally retarded, and it has proven invaluable for those with severe speech problems. Burger deals extensively with the use of the pantomime and types such as the "mood" and the "change-of-mood" pantomime.

Role-Playing

Children learn about roles by actually performing them, but for some trainable children it will take a long time before they will take part in a very simple role game. John pretended he was a pastor, the other children imitated, and something was learned concerning the pastor.

Role-playing helps the trainable person become familiar with and remember events, ideas and situations occurring in a story, poem, etc. Actually, almost any kind of experience may be acted out and become the subject for role-playing, which gives repeated opportunities for development of speech of all kinds. It also helps to develop self-control.[12] Role-playing helps the frustrated retarded person to act out certain behavioral characteristics. If a pupil demonstrates his feelings and frustrations in the role-playing situation, he affords his teacher a better opportunity to understand him and his individual needs.

For this activity the church school teacher can use simple Bible stories, limiting the number of participants to three or four. Before "playing" the story, there should be what Alan Klein terms "briefing and warming up."[13] The trainable person needs exceptionally clear instructions and repetition, and it may take a considerable length of time to get him to participate, but once the method is begun it will prove invaluable as a teaching method. Simple Bible stories can be "acted out" by the students, for example, they can all help lift "Baby Moses" out of the water, and through this dramatic activity they are able to learn from each other.

Puppetry

Since trainable mentally retarded persons find great joy in the use of puppetry, the feeling of spontaneity, of talking out problems with no fear of censure of ideas, thoughts and concepts, can be developed with the use of puppets in the church school.[14] An important goal of the trainable mentally retarded is socialization, and great strides toward this goal can be achieved through puppetry. Frequently the activity helps pupils to release frustration, thus reducing tension within and without.

The most essential element in using puppetry is the flexibility of approach. The experiences of the children are brought into action, their language ability — clarity and fluidity of speech — is increased, and they learn more about the Bible. The teacher must realize that biblical concepts can be effectively taught through the use of puppets. Teachers accused of "wasting time" with puppetry are certainly falsely accused, for the children bring to their puppets feelings of love, understanding and enthusiasm.

With greater insight into the trainable mentally retarded, and a new view toward the child's mind and emotions, we are coming to realize that he is a creative personality. Slowly our educational tools are being adapted in order to benefit every child, and the church also must recognize these new methods. Once the teacher observes how puppetry aids the mentally retarded in both learning and encouraging spiritual growth, he will be more eager to use it.[15]

Visual Aids

PICTURES

The teacher should make use of visuals in achieving his goals, and one of the most valuable and versatile visuals is the picture. Flat pictures are the oldest, the least expensive, and the most universally available of all materials of instruction. Pictures seldom add new dimensions to the learning, but they reinforce or illustrate the learning, so they can be used to define and set limits rather than serve as bridges to new relationships.[16]

The church school teacher should capitalize on the familiar, selecting pictures for his retarded class to help pupils recall their own related experiences. Pictures also can correct false conceptions which pupils hold, as well as prevent misconceptions. They can give a drab classroom a more attractive appearance, although too many pictures will disturb the hyperactive retarded person. Pictures used in the church school prove invaluable in showing behavior patterns, thus aiding the retarded in his relationship to others as well as in his own behavior patterns.

Williams lists certain characteristics of good pictures for effective classroom purposes:
1. Sharp point (lesson aim)
2. Present a unified arrangement
3. Convey truthful impressions
4. Reproduce color accurately
5. Suit the picture-reading ability of the learner.[17]

The retarded have a low level of conceptualizing and generalizing; therefore, the pictures must meet both the mental and chronological age of the retarded.

The alert Sunday school teacher will place himself in a position to recognize potentially useful picture material. Magazines represent a vast source of study pictures which should be utilized. Louis Rosenzweig and Julia Long suggest colored pictures of things familiar to the retarded, such as food, clothing, animals, toys, people — boy, girl members of the family.[18] Also, books can be an important source of excellent picture materials.

EXHIBITS

Exhibits, which can show a variety of materials related to a unit of work, should be considered an integral part of the given unit and planned in such a way that they contribute to the solution of problems that may have arisen in class. Certain guidelines should be followed for more effective learning:

1. Do not clutter the exhibit. Retarded persons, especially hyperactive, feel a certain uneasiness in complexity.

2. Place the most important objects in strategic positions.

3. Allow the students to help in the planning and development of the exhibit.

4. Give attention to eye level; secure effective lighting.

5. Discuss the exhibits with the students.

Other visual-aid resources that can be used effectively are blackboards, charts, marionettes, models, murals, objects, posters, slides, filmstrips and maps. All these must be used in a most simplified form, yet advanced enough to satisfy the differing needs.

CREATIVE ART

David is retarded but, happy and content, takes crayon in hand and begins to draw. His crayon moves about on the paper without association with an idea. He paints a line and calls it a dog; the next minute the same line is a house. Perhaps he draws Mommy with legs dangling from a pudgy body, and he may even include facial features.

The Sunday school teacher should use large, thick crayons, blunt scissors, or double-handled scissors. Paints should be tube water colors which are dissolved in small cans, each with its own brush. (Long-handled brushes with thick bristles are good.) This eliminates washing brushes, a task too difficult for the trainable child. Fortunately, it also preserves paints.

Expression and mood indicate individuality, and research has proven that trainable children possess the capacity to express their feelings pictorially.

How often have you been called upon to explain something in compelling terms and found yourself inadequate? Retarded persons feel inadequacy much more keenly, for they have fewer words and far less confidence. How can we assist them? Although retarded persons are not creative in the general sense, they love crafts because this handwork peculiarly satisfies some of their unexpressed needs. Therefore, the teacher should expose a retarded pupil to various materials and let him express himself as well as he is able, always being careful not to judge him according to adult standards, but by his own individual scale of development.

Typical of all human beings, the retardate gains a feeling of confidence and self-satisfaction through the simple task of making something himself. Therefore, the church school teacher must be sensitive to the ability of his pupil in order that the pupil may experience confidence and achievement through the medium of art.

The teacher must show the retarded how to do things. It is not sufficient merely to give verbal directions, but he must reinforce them by actually helping the child with his project. Guiding his hands and assisting him in his movement are necessary requisites for the teacher of trainables. However, he should not help when the pupil is capable of doing things for himself.

Objectives given for arts and crafts for the trainable mentally retarded person have been developed by Eleanor M. Healy:

1. To help the retarded child to find joy and satisfaction in expressing himself.
2. To develop creativity by providing a stimulating art program which will achieve expression and success for the mentally retarded child.
3. To develop manipulative skills by experience with many art processes and materials.
4. To sustain and nurture an awareness of the world about us.[19]

The church school teacher will add a fifth objective: To develop spiritual growth in the life of the retarded.

These objectives can only be achieved when the teacher's planning is careful, for he can only foster spiritual development by correlating arts and crafts with the lesson. Much of the printed church school curriculum material is not suitable for use with the retarded because as the chronological age and physical age of the retarded increase, the mental age stays on a much more even keel, bringing added problems to art expression.‖

Natalie Perry gives some suggestions for using crafts:

1. The craft should be useful.
2. The craft should be simple enough to learn with detailed instruction and practice.
3. The craft should be one that can be done outside of school.
4. A simple craft should be at least one more step toward learning a more useful craft.
5. The craft should be of interest to the child.[20]

The teacher must remember that their capacities are limited, and their perseverance spasmodic. However, their delight in what they have been able to express is unbounded and their satisfaction in its completion is its own reward.

CREATIVE MUSIC ACTIVITIES

Whatever the trainable mentally retarded is presently learning can be emphasized, and past experiences can be reviewed, by the use of music.[21] The value of music in varied forms can scarcely be overestimated, for through it may come the release of pent-up emotions, the development of an innate ability on the part of some, and the sheer joy of singing, playing or listening by everyone. It creates a pleasant atmosphere, provides security, stimulates imagination, and helps to develop the vocabulary.

Most mentally retarded persons enjoy singing, even

‖ Practically nothing has been done by the church to provide arts and crafts for older persons, especially the adolescent. The authors, experimenting with coloring, enlisted the help of a student artist, Margie Bodle, to draw pictures of fashionable ladies for her female students to color. It was observed during the year that these were preferred by her students in the twenties. One student refused all coloring, except the fashion pictures. A fleeting observation was made that the higher the level of the trainable, the more conscious they were of doing "baby" pictures or activities. The authors feel the "educable" would profit most from specifically designed materials.

though some may be limited to humming a tune. The person's ability in this area usually exceeds his academic ability, but great care must be taken lest the retarded become overstimulated.[22] For example, in an early experience with music, a rhythm band's effects were noticed; during one session a usually stable student passed out with an epileptic seizure due to overstimulation. If any part of the music program causes the person to become excited, its use must be discontinued until the group can handle it.

Conversely, the use of music can play a constructive emotional role, for it helps create within the person a mood or attitude conducive to better functioning and learning. Soft, slow music may calm an excitable child or quiet a noisy group.‡

The teacher himself should personally enjoy a music session and his enjoyment should be obvious to the students, for then he is more likely to foster this feeling of enjoyment and well-being among his students.

Music serves a variety of other purposes:

1. Setting a mood.
2. Auditory training.
3. As a tool for learning.
4. Opportunity for social growth.
5. Physical growth.
6. Spiritual growth.[23]

Cruickshank suggests steps in using music that may be helpful to the Sunday school teacher if he is to help the mentally retarded gain maximum spiritual growth. In the beginning, quiet music might be played, perhaps hymns of a soothing nature on a record player. Rhythms may be used to de-

---

‡ Music is also used by experts as a psychotherapeutic approach to the trainable mentally retarded. This is now considered within the province of the classroom teacher. Knight and his co-workers point out that when properly used, it will enable the retarded child to inhibit his random muscular impulses. For more information, consult D. Knight, A. J. Ludwig and L. Pope, "The Role of Varied Therapies in the Rehabilitation of the Retarded Child," *American Journal of Mental Deficiency* 61 (1957): 508-15.

velop a feeling for fast and slow, loud and soft, and pupils can
be shown how to clap noiselessly. Music has a great potential
for teaching more than sound discrimination, for it can provide
individual therapy if handled skillfully. Music can promote
relaxation and provide an ever broadening field of recreation
for the person as he acquires a joy and feeling for music.[24]

SONGS

Singing is the expression of happiness and joyful hearts
that are finding themselves. What better place than the
church school to encourage expressions of happiness, regardless of quality? Since part-singing and sight-reading are beyond the ability of these pupils, the best approach is by rote
— by repetition and imitation. The teacher must know the
song well and teach one or two lines at a time.

Thus, in selection of music, Perry gives criteria which
should be noted when choosing songs for use in the church
school's "special class":

1. Simple. . . . Melody should usually not be longer than
   twelve measures, with repetitious phrases and a very
   limited range of notes.
2. Familiar or natural sounding. . . . The vocabulary and
   sentence forms ought to be those in common usage and
   arranged in a natural way of speaking.
3. Clear. . . . The rhythm should have prominent beats emphasized a little more than ordinarily.
4. Slow in tempo. . . . The mentally retarded need time to
   sing the words.
5. Interesting and stimulating in melody, rhythm, and language, but not too exciting.
6. Educational. . . . (For the church school it must have a
   definite Christian emphasis).
7. Meeting a wide range of needs.[25]

With these criteria in mind, one must be careful even in
the use of commonly used (not always acceptable) songs in
the church school. Choruses are a source of delight; however,

caution must be used and good judgment applied in the selection.

Essentially, the retarded are concerned with the world in which they move. Whatever appeals to the five senses has reality, such as songs referring to birds, flowers, sun, moon or stars, which make the love and care of God significant to them.

Little spiritual value will be derived from even the simplest of songs unless the teacher first introduces the meaning of the words in the pupils' own terms. Since it is difficult to find short and simple hymns which meet the retarded adolescent's needs and experiences, illustrated hymns should be used to clarify meaning and encourage worship experiences.

MUSIC LISTENING

The phonograph and the radio are both valuable as means of assistance and inspiration in the development of music appreciation. Records may be used by the entire group at one time or by individuals as they are in the mood for it. Also, a record playing helps when one is using music for a story background. Correlation with the experiences of the day is desirable here, as in all other fields of art. If tied to the main theme, the message will carry over far more effectively into the life of the retarded.**

RHYTHMS

Because most retarded children can learn to play and to enjoy playing a variety of rhythm instruments, a rhythm band is a good way of getting expression from them.[26] This provides lessons in teamwork and gives the child a sense of rhythm. Begin rhythm band activities by using sticks only. Later other instruments can be introduced, keeping one principle in mind: never discard the clap-hand motion. Instruments that need

---

** Records designed for the handicapped can be used only if they enhance the goals for the church school teacher. Examples of these are: "Creative Music for Exceptional Children," Classroom Materials, Inc., Merrick, New York; "Rhythms and Songs for Exceptional Children," Classroom Materials, Inc., Merrick, New York; "Songs for Children with Special Needs," Bowman Records, North Hollywood, California.

only one hand should be held and tapped against the palm of the other hand or against another stick. Instruments in the rhythm band can include drums (bongo, stick, Indian, steel), triangles, sticks, castanets, cymbals, bird whistles, xylophones, tambourines, maracas, long gourd, temple bells, and blocks, piccolo, harmonica.[27] Since it is more difficult for retarded persons to shake just one hand in a rhythmic manner, the contact with the other hand establishes control and aids the child's coordination.

8

How Shall the Family Be Counseled Regarding Problems of Retardation?

A CHILD IS BORN RETARDED. Many cases are now diagnosed within hours of birth, so parents hear almost immediately that their newborn is retarded. Other parents hear the truth only after gnawing fears have materialized into the agonizing truth that their child is retarded. For many the shock is so great that their bundle of joy turns to horror. They plead, "What is it? Why? What can you do about it, Doctor?" He has very few answers, and they carry their baby home from the hospital or doctor's office — mystified and hurt.

Learning about mental retardation is an emotional shock that brings total involvement with a deformed and defective human being. To some it is the same as death. After the initial shock, the full realization overwhelms parents and piles up emotions of shame, guilt, frustration, confusion, bitterness, envy, rejection of the child, or insistence that the child is normal.[1] Some parents immediately seek medical help, seeing doctor after doctor, hoping to be told that their baby will mature normally. Others refuse any kind of medical help because they are not ready to face the truth about retardation.

The tragedy of mental retardation strikes the parents much harder than it does the child, for the more retarded the child, the less he realizes his condition. Parents could face the truth if society, and particularly Christian society, could be realistic and loving about human weakness. The reverse is

92

true of many who hide deficiencies to give the impression that the child is perfect, hoping no one will recognize the retardation. Unfortunately, the plan never works out in practice. Weakness does come to the surface, where dealing with it is inescapable. Nonetheless, it is an extremely painful experience because retardation is starkly real and devastating to a family.

The shock of retardation will be greater in the family where parents place a high value on education and achievement, for retardates can only attain semiskilled-worker status, and that only after extensive and patient training. Parents may need extensive counseling before they relinquish hopes of a higher education for their child, but those who accept mental retardation as a fact sometimes find a new kind of joy in nurturing the child for what he is.

Retarded children probably feel more acceptance in the lower-economic-level family, in which complete education is the goal of only a few. Jenny, who had an IQ of 70, was born into a miner's family whose needs were met through daily hard work on everyone's part. Jenny was, of course, different, but her failure to perform as well as other members of the family did not make her an outcast in the family or community. Her handicap was totally accepted, though not understood.

> When parents discover at birth or later that their baby is retarded, it is bound to be a shock to them. In a way, they may feel they are different. Parents seem to lose their identity for a while. It takes time to get used to this different person they've become and to see and accept the new person their baby has become. How the parents feel about having a retarded child is basic to everything that happens to him and his family.[2]

It is possible that the news may come as a relief. If the parents have suspected something to be wrong for some time and have felt themselves to be failing as parents they may react quite differently. Pressure from relatives and friends often adds to this feeling. The diagnosis would then offer a measure of relief from such confusion.[3]

Another shock comes if parents decide they must institutionalize a retarded child or adult. The reasons for and against institutionalization are not equal, and every family must base the decision on its own needs. However, it is an extremely difficult task to institutionalize a family member, as necessary as it may be. A middle-aged couple had raised their family and the last son was attending college. They had planned at this point in life to sell their urban home and travel, and then live a kind of pioneer existence in the country. This had been a lifelong dream. One of their children was trainably retarded, and had required continual care and supervision since birth. Now at twenty-five years, this severely handicapped daughter would not fit into future plans. Beyond that, she must have care if she outlived her parents.

This was a logical time to consider institutionalization. Other family members should be free for marriage and careers rather than making a home for the handicapped person. However, counselors and friends should never underestimate the emotional drain of parting with the retarded child or adult, as difficult as caring for him might have been.

Emotionally healthy parents can survive the shock of parting with their retarded child, but not every couple is well adjusted. For the chronically disturbed parent (e.g., the one who needs a "cross to bear" to maintain a neurotic adjustment to himself and others), separation is traumatic. The parent may have found in the retarded child a "new meaning in life," or a focal point for activity and endeavor; thus, he may become more dependent on the child than the child is on him, and to institutionalize the child would be taking away the "crutch." The suffering involved in "bearing the cross" may be more easily borne than the anxiety which would be aroused in assuming responsibility for his own happiness and behavior. The more the child is used as a psychological crutch by the parent, the more he becomes a part of the parent's total psychological functioning, the greater will be the difficulties in working with the parent toward his best interests.[4]

Often the parents of the mildly retarded child desire their child to "catch up," and they fall into the delusion that their child is only a "slow learner." Since the condition of the severely retarded is so obvious, this problem doesn't arise. Also, the physical handicap makes the mental retardation easier to accept.

It is impossible to categorize the kinds of shock that the parents undergo. For example, if the parents are told at the time of birth, their "expectancy" is shattered, for most parents have been building toward a climax and such a pronouncement is like a pin piercing their balloon of dreams. All too often they have had no contact with the mentally retarded or, at any rate, are devoid of any knowledge concerning them. It is not uncommon for parents to discover there is much to love and that this child, though mentally deficient, can still bring joy to their home. Another kind of shock centers around the parents' system of values. If they place high value on achievement and education, certainly the fact that their child will only be semiskilled brings a shock to them. Whereas the "expectancy shock" requires supportive counseling and information, this latter "value shock" will require a reevaluation on the part of the parents.

Parents have a second reaction to retardation, that of guilt. It can be so deep and misunderstood that it blocks all constructive thinking for and about the child, such as his status in the family, needed therapy and schooling possibilities. Guilt arises in parents for many reasons: they may see retardation as God's punishment for such sins as not wanting the child in the first place, attempting abortion, permissive sex before marriage, or for any number of other real or imagined sins.

The counselor's first job will be to deal with and help resolve guilt. Since parents usually will want to do little to help the retarded person if they intend to accept it as punishment for sin, counselors must emphasize God's willingness to forgive all sin and to take away all guilt (1 Jn 1:9).

Guilt may be the reason why some parents overprotect their retarded child. Secretly they may desire to disown him, but they overcompensate for this secret desire by smothering him with attention and keeping him from any possible harm. Perhaps he would be able to learn self-care and other skills — the things which would bring him pride and some self-assurance — but parents fear for his safety, and thereby condemn him to a much worse life than necessary.

Frustration is a common reaction which may result from a number of obstacles which mount, causing increased tension. Some of these may include lack of services, funds, social stigma, slow maturation, and a feeling that the parent will not "live on" in the child since it is unlikely that the child will marry.

ROLES OF THE CHURCH AND PASTOR

If the church truly does wish to have a ministry to "all the world," it will educate itself to the needs of the retarded and their families. The foregoing discussion reveals the broken and vulnerable state of mind of the new parents of retarded children. The church must be ready to administer spiritual and emotional healing for parents expect help, and they have a right to. Even as they plead with the doctor, "What are you going to do to help my baby?"[5] they also have the right to ask the church, "What are *you* going to do to help me?"

> We are at the dawning of a new era of sympathy and understanding; yet unquestionably, our parents have a right to think religious training can make and is making a big contribution in this direction.[6]

The determined church can surround parents with understanding and various forms of moral support, such as assuring each family member of a secure place in the church. This may mean forming a special class for the retardate.

The worker with retarded pupils should play a role of supportive friend and counselor if he is ready for the responsibility. He may not have always been involved with the parents of retarded children. One survey shows that of 220 clergymen of various Christian denominations, 90 percent felt the church was responsible for the religious care of the retarded and that this was possible. Only a minority, however, indicated that they had ever been in a counseling situation with a retardate or his family. Those who had been involved tended to characterize this as "pastoral care," in other words, short-term, unstructured consultation.[7] Church workers can be reluctant to counsel families of the retarded because (1) they feel they need training in mental health before they can be helpful, and (2) because the needs of retarded persons are unknown to them.[8] These needs are very real. Two factors will enhance a teacher's ability to counsel the problems of retardation: (1) Families will want information of medical and educational resources. Perhaps the teacher himself will have to find initial information by searching the telephone book of the largest nearby city. (2) The teacher will need to take adequate time with parents facing retardation. They will work out their feelings slowly, and they will need week by week, year by year patient understanding from their pastor (or lay church worker with retarded children).[9] Parents want to know that the teacher accepts their feelings, and is willing to participate in their struggles.

Counseling Parents

Compassion communicates to both parents and children. A family doesn't feel alone when a Christian teacher is standing by, trying to share their despair. Perhaps the teacher is knowledgeable enough only to listen and sympathize, or perhaps he can offer a deeper psychological help which some parents will require. Wherever his counseling talents lie, the teacher first must reveal that he really cares. He must counter through his compassion two attitudes generally felt by families of the retarded: (1) fear and indifference toward retardation in the community, and (2) being treated as a case history in the medical world. Parents need to express all of their feelings — the despair and the hope — to someone who will listen and not be judgmental.

Parents will request two kinds of advice from the Christian teacher. First, help for themselves; and second, sources of help for their child. Spiritually, they first react by doubting God's goodness, for the blame for retardation is usually placed on God. Even if a couple receives retardation as punishment, it can drive them farther away from God as they question His love for them: "He wouldn't do this to us if He really cared!" Some questions are theological: "If God is good, how can He allow helpless babies to come into the world with such handicaps? Does He really care? Why did He let this happen to us? What sin have we committed that has caused God to punish us this way?" Other normal concerns about the child: "Are we expecting too much or too little from him? What does the future hold for him?"[10]

The family pastor will be an immense help to turn their thoughts from such questions to more constructive thinking, such as building toward the child's future. Some of these disturbing questions do not have easy or immediate answers. The wise counselor will not attempt to be God to them but will redirect them until they are able to think more objectively. Perhaps they may then be able to see how much the child can do for them in building strength of character.

> Many parents when faced with this severe disappointment in their personal lives, lose faith in themselves and their ability to cope with a problem which they realize

will never have a final and permanent solution so long as the child lives. Worse than this, they lose faith in God as a God of love, of mercy and justice. The clergyman who can lead them to a stage of spiritual maturity that enables them to see life as still worth living and God as still loving and worthy of being loved, has done his part of the job — and done it well.[11]

There are not many families that have not suffered from some deviation from the normal. If mental retardation could be placed at the door of iniquity on the part of some member of the family, we would have mentally retarded children in every family.[12]

A counseling ministry may be a harder test of a teacher's durability than teaching retarded children, for families sometimes turn their back on God when retardation hits and do not welcome church help. For example, Ellen and Jack Hagan permitted their retarded son to go to church school with a neighboring family, but wanted no contact with the church themselves. The pastor, deacons and special education teacher tried contacting them — with no success. But a breakthrough came when the little boy became school age and the Hagans were fearful and unsure of his eligibility for public school. Also, they feared looking into the matter, which had to be faced. Finally they accepted an invitation to the fellowship group of their son's church school class. Parents gathered informally on a Saturday for a picnic supper simply to share problems and victories, bringing all of their children and making it a social occasion for the whole family.

The Hagans came to this gathering hoping for answers about where their son could go to school, and this need alone kept them coming to the group month after month. As the relationship deepened, they began to feel the need to attend church and eventually to become Christians. But for the pastor and his church, this was (and is) a long-term ministry.

One aspect of healthy adjustment to retardation involves

the parents' own relationship, for if a couple has lived together successfully before the birth of a retarded child, they are likely to continue living in harmony. At first they will feel the shock, dismay and fear experienced by everyone in that situation, and they will need medical advice about their child. The sympathy of their church can cushion the shock; beyond that, they have the inner resources to reorganize their thinking and live in peace together. However, the retarded who is born into an already troubled home tends to compound and deepen all of the problems.

The medical advice to be given parents would include getting the diagnosis first, in other words, a complete evaluation. Then they should put their faith in the physician whose opinion and judgment they value; they should be discouraged from running from one physician to another. Parents will help their child most by being realistic, not trying to overrate his ability, and by following the medical program laid out by the physician.[13]

Parents need help with feelings to assure their own health and happiness and because their attitudes have such an impact on the other children in the home. When shame and guilt grip parents about retardation, the children assume the same life-style. Perhaps the parents had never lived normally as grownups themselves, or the complete reverse is possible. For example, one boy became so attached to his retarded sister during their childhood that he found it difficult parting with her in his college years. Their home had been full of love and acceptance, even for the severely handicapped member.

Counselors should urge parents to educate themselves and their children about the needs and abilities of retarded persons, for they all need to understand the problem, and they will, in turn, be able to confidently handle questions coming from friends and acquaintances. Parents who cover up the problem only make it difficult for the entire family to make a healthy life adjustment.

The question is frequently asked concerning the time to tell the siblings of the retarded child and what they should and should not be told. The answer to this question depends upon the siblings' reactions to the child. If they notice something is wrong, they should be told the truth; it is certainly better than hearing it from neighbors or friends.

The effects of the retarded child upon siblings varies and it may safely be said that their adjustment is neither better nor worse because of it, when compared to other children in general. Generally the youngsters are able to make adequate adjustment around the retarded sibling. If problems do arise, they usually are traced to the attitudes of the parents, so it is wiser to plan counseling around the parent than the sibling.

Education about retardation includes full knowledge of a child's abilities and disabilities. Parents should set standards and goals for the retarded child below those of the other children, and then be careful not to compare achievements. Since the retarded has deep feelings about his inadequacies, the most helpful thing anyone can do is to set up situations in which he can succeed. Never pressure him to do a task perfectly, but praise him abundantly for whatever effort he makes.

Those who counsel parents about achievement for their retarded children should remember the paradox with which parents live every day. They know the truth; doctors have told them, but they go on hoping. One couple said concerning their little boy, "His growth did not increase as we had hoped, but his awkwardness became more apparent. But in the quiet moments when he snuggled in our arms, we sensed that in his thin little frame there was a beautiful little boy longing to be freed."[14] It is through this kind of hope that parents help an injured child live at his potential.

The counselor may need to help the family in these additional areas:

1. *Give other children the quality of care and attention*

received by the retardate. Equal time for each child may not be possible, especially if retardation is severe; however, parents must find ways to show other children that they do not love them any less, such as by planning vacations and special days without the retardate. Parents may rightfully consider institutionalization of the brain-damaged youngster who leaves them absolutely no time for normal family living.

2. *Do not push a child beyond his capabilities to the point of frustration.* Because pushing only tends to destroy any healthy emotional balance the retardate has attained, parents must trust his schoolteachers and go along with their advice about his expected rate of improvement. Always praise his effort.

3. *Do not pauperize the family to give the retarded child the best.* Resentment will only build in the family. Some states have passed legislation providing a monthly allowance to parents of the mentally retarded. Illinois passed such a bill in 1969 which covers medical expenses, food, shelter, and personal needs.[15]

4. *Do not be afraid to have other children.* Nothing heals the hurt of having a retarded baby more than the birth of a normal child.[16] It can take away much self-doubt, restoring respect and confidence to a marriage. One mother put her feelings into words: "Secretly we blamed each other for our retarded child. Then Jonathan was born. We didn't plan to have him, and I actually dreaded the day of his birth, thinking that we would face another disappointment. The wedge in our marriage would be driven deeper. But we had a healthy boy. He has changed many things for my husband and me, and in our home."

Some couples just do not want other children for many reasons, including the desire to devote their total time to the handicapped child. Counselors may need to thoroughly evaluate a family's emotional, psychological and financial readiness before encouraging the parents to have more children.

5. *Urge participation in parents' groups for retardation.* The counselor should go so far as to find out where these groups are located and when they meet. Through such groups, parents will learn much more than any teacher could ever tell them about the facts of retardation. Also, these groups would welcome the pastor or church teacher who wishes more education about retardation.

There is a danger on the part of professionals to treat the parents of mentally retarded children as members of one category and, in so "lumping" them, fail to realize their individuality. But each case is different, with unique problems and unique personalities involved. While their reactions may be of the same type, they still retain their individuality.

Some will make an adequate adjustment, while others have had psychological difficulties which come to the forefront when such a crisis occurs. Their adjustment will be considerably different and will require care reflecting this unique therapeutic situation.

One must remain aware of the multiple determinates of behavior. There are those who are devoid of happiness and have been searching for peace and security; they have been lonely or have had unsatisfactory interpersonal relationships.[17]

An excellent summary to a chapter on counseling parents of mentally retarded children is one given by Levinson, who calls these "The 10 Commandments for Parents of Retarded Children":

1. Get medical advice early and follow the programs outlined.
2. Don't adopt a defeatist attitude.
3. Don't develop a complex of shame or guilt.
4. Don't neglect your normal children because of your retarded child.
5. Don't pauperize yourself to give your child the best.
6. Don't push your child beyond his capabilities.
7. Try to meet your child's emotional needs.

8. Don't be afraid to have other children.
9. Do not covet the child of your neighbor.
10. Help further the cause of the mentally retarded.[18]*

9

How Should the Retarded Person Be Counseled?

SUCCESSFUL COUNSELORS with the retarded have the two prime requirements of (1) a knowledge of brain damage, and (2) a positive, healthy attitude toward these persons and their problems. Therefore, not every lay or professional person should attempt to counsel the retarded, for the retarded can regress emotionally by wrong counseling techniques. The retarded feel warmth, love and acceptance in the same way as normal pupils, and with just as much depth. Rejection also hits them forcefully and more frequently. Few people are quick to accept the worth of a brain-damaged child or adult, but acceptance is the key to his well-being.

The counselor must be positive, realizing God has a plan for each retarded person. God's purpose in the life of retarded students adds meaning and enjoyment to our ministry with them.

> The retarded child, like each normal child, is sent by God for a purpose which no one else can accomplish. The prime life purpose is to give glory to God by fulfilling His plan — a plan which is far better than any humanly devised idea. This purpose is attained through individual capacity, and it varies greatly from person to person. Christianity recognizes the worth of every human life, no matter how feebly it functions.[1]

It would be an oversight to imply that there are no great problems connected with counseling the retarded child, some of which involve theory, approach, goals and methods. Space permits discussing only a few, and no attempt is made to be exhaustive.

The question has been raised whether the retarded are even suitable for counseling, since some people claim that they do not possess the necessary ego-resources for positive growth. Should they be kept separate from normal children or should they be allowed to integrate? When considering the retardate's acceptance of himself, should a counselor strive to produce self-assurance and competence, or should he try to produce "good people" who realize their limitations? Perhaps the answer to the last question might be that we strive to achieve both. A significant statement by Jordan gives direction: "It has been shown that psychotherapy for the retarded can produce a positive change in the level and manner of behavior."[2]

Therefore, counseling can make a difference in the mentally retarded. Their life can be upgraded and their life direction changed.

Counselor Qualifications

In this discussion of counselor qualifications, a positive attitude must precede all other factors. To this thesis, the Reverend Vernon Lyons, whose church* ministers to eighteen retarded children and their families, agrees. He states that integration of brain-damaged children into the church family "has been no problem because the congregation seeks to diminish the differences between people." Retarded persons in Ashburn Baptist Church have their own Sunday school class, worship service, weekday clubs and prayer meeting.

The counselor can be anyone from a professional to lay person who is obviously capable of supporting and building self-esteem in the retarded. The untrained person sometimes has this supportive ability, which may be enhanced under

---

* Ashburn Baptist Church, 3647 W. 83rd Street, Chicago.

supervision, but supervision is not always essential for good results. The natural expression of love can be a prime qualification to counsel, but not all loving persons are trained enough to help the retarded.

What are the qualifications that a counselor should have to care for the retardate and the family? Would anyone with counseling experience qualify? This is hardly the case, for certain unique features must be considered before a person is qualified.

Wolfensberger lists ten qualifications for the counselor:

1. Knowledge of the aspects of retardation.
2. Knowledge of resources.
3. Competency in techniques of counseling.
4. Experience in the applied clinical areas of retardation.
5. Freedom from stereotypes about retardation.
6. Positive attitudes toward retardation.
7. Orientation to the current community-centered management approach.
8. Sensitivity to the reality needs of the family.
9. Willingness to go beyond the traditional approaches to help the parents.
10. Patience.[3]

From the above, the most striking qualification which makes this counseling unique is not only knowledge of the retarded but positive attitudes toward the person as well. The counselor may be unaware of some of these until he is brought face to face with an individual situation. This thought is amplified by Wolfensberger when he states three counselor-centered obstacles which have barred the way to effective work with parents:

1. Viewing the parents as "patients" and seeing the source of the problem as residing with them.
2. Deep-seated attitudes toward defect and retardation that are basically no different than those often held by the parents themselves or by the community at large.

3. Many individuals who counsel parents, even if free of detrimental attitudes and backgrounds, have had little training or experience in mental retardation or even in normal child development. They feel inadequate in managing practical problems and therefore restrict counseling too often to stereotyped discussions of parental feelings.[4]

Teachers counsel more with the retarded than do other professionals because they spend more time with the children than anyone else except parents. Michael came to his primary Sunday school class over a year before he would do any more than stand by the door and observe. Teachers greeted him and treated him warmly but never insisted that he participate. They invited him to join in but never tried to force his involvement. Finally one Sunday he felt secure enough to leave his place at the door to sit down and worship with his classmates. Michael had taken a major step in his growth. Thus, ministry to the retarded takes simple, basic steps based on the knowledge that they need a great deal of patient help in forming acceptable behavior habits.

Elements of a Counseling Ministry

A good counseling relationship with the retarded involves portions of the following elements: establishing a warm, accepting climate; setting boundaries; expressing and clarifying feelings; supplying encouragement, support and motivation; interpreting feelings and giving advice.[5]

More important than the technique he uses is the rapport that he is able to establish with the retarded. He must make an honest effort to understand, to see the situation from their perspective. Most importantly, he must genuinely like them. He must have the inner conviction that they are worthwhile, that their problems, their feelings, their needs are important, that they are significant in the eyes of God.[6]

1. *Acceptance.* Perhaps acceptance is the reason why teachers do the most effective counseling. They have learned to love and accept the children through daily contact with them and, also through daily contact, they have discovered undesirable characteristics which must be dealt with on the spot. Teachers learn to do this and still show love.

Acceptance can be the most powerful kind of technique with the retarded because it deals with their most basic need to belong. Because they experience constant rejection and rebuff, they need genuine friendship from a counselor who has the inner conviction that they are significant to God and to man.[7]

God puts emphasis on the positive side of life, urging us to do the right and good thing, and forgiving and forgetting our negative behavior. This should be a counselor's strategy with the retarded. The retarded feels acceptance when you compliment him for a good thing he does. He behaves negatively primarily because people expect him to do the wrong thing; thus he feels compelled to meet their expectations by acting badly. One key to helping him is to accept his simple, awkward efforts and always offer abundant praise.

The normal person has trouble accepting his own deficiencies, sometimes making the best use of his strong points only after someone has helped him understand what they are. The retarded has such a low self-image that he must be taught to love and respect himself. This can be done by de-emphasizing intellectual deficiency and showing genuine appreciation for strengths.

2. *Setting boundaries.* Most professionals come to a counseling situation with definite dos and don'ts or rules for the patient to follow, for example, they cannot kick, bite or scratch the counselor. The lay counselor should adapt the same attitude, for his self-worth must be respected just as he respects the "growing person" in the retarded. The retarded

must know what is expected of him; the counselor should not allow for laziness or less than a conscious effort.

Setting boundaries when counseling primarily means limiting the child's aggressive behavior, as well as choosing topics and directing the conversation. The aggressive behavior is both why the child gets the teacher's attention and why he needs counsel. Eight-year-old Randy (IQ 75) reacts violently when his teacher invites him to join in class activity. No wonder; his parents criticize his every deed. Randy is completely frustrated, having never succeeded in pleasing his parents, so now he is afraid of disappointing his teacher also and he escapes by having a tantrum.

Counseling in this kind of situation demands more than the accepted techniques. The teacher must first gain the child's attention and confidence, perhaps by holding him physically until he vents his anger, and then speaking softly, hoping to calm him.

Another kind of counseling boundary takes place during classroom activity. Pamela is severely retarded; she is quiet and makes no effort to respond, even with eye contact. She refuses to do anything. The teacher decides that her boundary for further help depends on whether Pamela walks up and deposits her collection money. The teacher helps her meet that requirement by bodily walking her to the pulpit and depositing the coins. She has succeeded (though with assistance), and the counseling situation continues with the teacher's praise, "Good girl, Pamela."

Teachers and counselors can remain calm when facing a child's outbursts if they understand that the anger is only a symptom of a root cause — the real problem which they can learn to treat effectively.

> Aggression is fashioned from experience; it is a learned reaction to frustration brought on by parental and social reward and punishment. If a child learns frustration in every part of life, each new frustration will further convince

him that things will always go wrong and readies him to respond violently. Thus he has few other responses available.[8]

Role-play is a technique for the untrained counselor to help the retarded child ventilate his emotions (see chap. 7 on teaching methods). Through role-play the children can vent feelings in a perfectly acceptable way, having imaginary quarrels with peers or superiors, and never suffering punishment when putting their hostility into the mouths of the characters they are playing. For instance, six-year-old Amy, who all along suspected that the teacher did not like her, was assigned the teacher role. Playing the teacher, Amy said, "I do not like Amy. I will not look at her or touch her. I will not smile at her." This child taught her teacher an important lesson, thus role-play can serve as a valuable counseling tool.

Since the retarded has difficulty responding to nondirective therapy, the lay counselor should choose the conversation topic and then usually direct its course. Professional therapists such as Carl Rogers, working with average persons, may use the nondirective method in which the counselor does not judge, nor direct conversation, or offer advice. He assumes that the patient can talk long enough to eventually understand his problems, and at some point bring about a comforting change.[9]

But the retarded has different problems. He rarely gets to his real problem until the counselor approaches the subject directly and then suggests direct action. Because these pupils have little insight for making decisions and also have little inhibitive control, they respond to both good and bad suggestions from the persons they fully trust. For example, nine-year-old retarded Joey has a two-year-old sister, Debbie, of normal intelligence who picks flowers, no matter where they are growing. Joey loves and trusts her; they entertain one another. His trust makes him go along with her suggestion to pick flowers, whether they are growing in the park or in the neighbor's yard. Their parents can quickly correct the bad habit with directive actions because Joey trusts them as much as he trusts Debbie, but a permissive atmosphere with Joey would be as useless as it would be with Debbie.

3. *Making decisions with the pupil's understanding for the decision.* Mrs. James called her primary class to order. Seven-year-old Franklin (IQ 70) decided not to cooperate that morning, preferring to continue his building-block project. She accepted his choice but stipulated that he would need to transfer his playthings into the hall so that her class activity would not be disturbed. Thus she approved his choice to play alone and then supported that choice by helping him move to the hall.

Mrs. James left Franklin alone and invited him to rejoin the class when he was ready. However, she knew that he would not be able to make that decision by himself. He would reach the point of wanting to join the other children but be unable to motivate himself to act. The teacher knew frustration would set in and that he would become angry and throw things. He did.

The noise alerted his teacher that Franklin needed help, so she went to him with definite goals — to help him understand and voice his feelings, to help him make a decision, and to support him in it. The conversation went something like this:

"Franklin, have you finished playing?"

No answer.

"I see that you're ready to come back to class."

The boy still doesn't answer but seems willing to drop his toys and return.

"Everyone would be happy if you come back with me. I would be happy too."

She aided his decision, but she also assisted his action. He stands there now with empty hands waiting to be led away. They enter the classroom hand in hand.

She encourages him: "Good boy, Franklin, we want you here with us."

She helped the boy do the thing he wanted to do all along but could not.

4. *Slow progress and repetition.* Since the retardate does have difficulty intellectualizing, it is important to check frequently on his understanding. Small steps should be taken, and great doses of patience are needed because understanding may only come after continuous repetition. It is possible for them to see themselves as they really are: limited. From this insight, valid goals can be assessed by the retardate and he may launch out to achieve these.

GOALS

Retarded persons are as much in need of guidance as any human beings. As a group they picture themselves repulsive and useless, for society has given them that role. No one pretends that their rehabilitation takes less than superhuman patience and love, but teachers and some parents do establish the necessarily simple goals, and then slowly work them into reality.

We have already implied that the counselor will set realistic goals for the retarded: (1) build a healthy self-concept, and (2) alter social behavior. Retardates can reach and retain these very basic goals, but their progress along the way will be painstakingly slow. This impeded progress is another reason why the special education teacher probably does the most effective counseling, for he keys himself to the pupil's improvement pace, always supporting and encouraging that improvement.

1. *Self-concept.* Retardates often dislike themselves and are frustrated by their limitations. Comparing themselves with people around them who have good physical ability and successful social interaction, they see that they do not measure

up. The crowd excludes them, others berate them. The opportunity to enjoy their own existence never comes. "Even in the retardation there is a strong motivation to become respected and responsible. A good counselor must believe in this, seek to establish the conditions wherein it may be nurtured and wait patiently."[10]

If there is any starting point with which to build an adequate self-concept it is found in the above quote. The retardate *does* have a desire for living as any other person, and this living is not merely an isolated existence but one of sharing with others in responsibility and social interaction.

> One of the goals of counseling is the development of a realistic, functional self-concept. The person who is handicapped must be helped to set realistic goals — both for the present and for the future. He needs to develop self-appreciation as well as appreciation of and respect for others.
>
> Through understanding his limitations and abilities we can anticipate problems he is sure to face and, through counseling, help prepare him to meet them. By helping him develop a functional self-concept we can help him learn to face the rebuffs, the condescension, the rejection of those who do not understand.[11]

Teachers in the church as well as public school should guarantee that a child feels good about himself in the classroom. The teacher must express total acceptance of the child and the things he does, never giving the retarded the opportunity to feel rejected because he acknowledges the child's presence enthusiastically, "Good morning, Henry. I'm glad that you're here. We have something special to do today." He can please his teacher, no matter how feeble are his efforts to do a task: "You have worked hard. I like what you have done." The pupil leaves there feeling like a worthwhile person who doesn't always have to fail. At least he has succeeded in making his teacher happy, and he begins to feel good about himself. Someone cared and supported his first steps toward a healthy self-concept.

Although the Christian counselor's major task is to build a proper self-concept in the retardate, this does not solve every problem but rather enables the person to have enough stability to handle these problems on his own and to maintain his equilibrium in the world. The importance of this cannot be overestimated, for "how he feels about himself may be more important in shaping his life than his intelligence."[12]

This may be accomplished by a loving concern and personal interest in him. Making him feel important involves giving him some responsibilities, something he can do that is "his job." In this way the sense of identity and belonging is developed for he becomes a part of this world rather than standing off and merely observing and being waited upon.

The responsibilty for helping a child build self-respect may fall on the pastor. For example, Melvin Oahrtman, chaplain of the Columbus State Schools which board the mentally retarded, frequently encounters the problem of parental rejection among the children, who often feel that since their family no longer wants them, that God also has turned His back.[13] Only a deep personal involvement with these children will restore self-confidence and faith in their heavenly Father. Admittedly this is an unsophisticated, simple kind of ministry, but it is exemplified by Christ's dealings with the poor and needy.

2. *Social behavior.* Retardates can fit into community life, whether into a family or institution, when they can approximate normal social behavior — not sophisticated behavior, just normal living. Thus the counselor works toward this goal, which is not as elusive as it may seem. The pupil wants to please those who give him love and care, and his family may not be filling this need. The teacher or counselor, who *does* genuinely love him, exerts tremendous positive effects on behavior when consciously working to do so.

Mr. Edwards, teacher of junior-age retarded children in public school, found this true in the case of twelve-year-old Brian who had an affinity for pencils. Brian routinely gathered up every pencil in sight and went looking through desks for more, a habit which distressed the entire class. Pupils spent the first five minutes of every period retrieving pencils.

Mr. Edwards was a Christian who tried to show God's love to his students, and in this case he alerted Brian's parents and Sunday school teacher about the problem. They agreed to the following approach: Criticizing Brian would do little good because it would bring negative belittling attention and give him further reason to behave badly. Rather, his teacher told Brian that everyone was displeased and hurt when he took things which did not belong to him. "God says, do not take things which belong to someone else. Brian, we love you. You hurt us when you take things. You hurt God, too."

Brian slowly gave up taking pencils. On occasion he would be tempted again, but Mr. Edwards knew that this battle for good behavior had been nearly won when Brian said one morning, "Mr. Edwards, I felt like taking some pencils this morning, but I remembered that God is watching me. I don't want to make Him sad. So I didn't even take one pencil." He grinned his self-approval.

SUMMARY

The counselor who helps a retarded student must consciously be aware of the pupil's limited abilities. Since the results will not be as profound and progress will come slowly over an extended period of time, the counselor may become easily discouraged. But being aware of the possibilities and the goals which can be attained, the counselor will realize that the approach will be simple and that patience coupled with extra skill are the primary requirements. The retarded has problems and feelings which will demand attention and concern, as would any counselee.

Appendix One

Historical Survey of Mental Retardation

IN REVIEWING the literature in the field of mental retardation, one becomes aware of the valuable contributions made in the field by such pioneers as Jean Marc Itard, Edward Seguin, and Marie Montessori. The work of these pioneers and their disciples during the nineteenth century may well be viewed as the first golden age for the mentally retarded pupil.[1]

Much progress has been made since the time when all mentally retarded children were believed to be possessed by demons which could only be expelled by magic and prayer. In ancient times the lot of the retarded was hopeless, the Spartans simply let them die of exposure. The earliest known patron, the fourth-century prelate, the Bishop of Myra, has been described as protector of the feebleminded; however, he is patron saint of all children and not qualified to figure in the chronicles of mental retardation.[2]

The rise of Christianity marked a gradual change in attitude. During the Christian era, the retarded were sheltered and treated much more humanely. The nineteenth century saw the problem of care and training of retarded individuals solved in a more scientific manner with such leaders as Itard, Seguin, Montessori and Decroly pioneering in what is now termed "special education."

Jean Marc Itard, a French philosopher (1774-1838), used methods of experimental psychology in attempting to teach or enculturate a retarded child.[3] He was inspired by the philosophy of sensationalism and the French postrevolutionary belief

117

that man had unlimited possibilities, and that education and environment were factors in mental development.[4]

In 1799 a boy about twelve years of age was captured in the forest of Aveyron in southern France. This boy, whom they called Victor, resembled a wild animal more than a human being. He was unable to speak, he selected his food by smell, attempted to escape, and in general did not respond like a human being. Reacting as an animal, he was consequently called "The Wild Boy of Aveyron." Itard felt that this boy was a good example of a completely untutored human being, and that with proper educational procedures applied to the training of the senses, this untutored boy could be made human.[5]

He embodied his program into five propositions:

1. To endear him to social life, by making it more congenial than the one he was now leading.
2. To awaken his nervous sensibility, by the most energetic stimulations; and at other times by quickening the affections of the soul.
3. To extend the sphere of his ideas, by creating new wants, and multiplying his associations with surrounding beings.
4. To lead him to the use of speech, by determining the exercise of imitation, under the spur of necessity.
5. To exercise the simple operations of his mind upon his physical wants, and therefrom derive the application of the same to objects of instruction.[6]

In 1802 he framed another program, more fitted for an idiot than a savage, whose foundation was physiological and whose generality embraced: (1) the development of the senses, (2) the development of the intellectual facilities, and (3) the development of the affective functions.[7]

Itard was successful in getting the boy to control his actions and read a few words by employing the basic rule of learning since posited by such learning theorists as Thorndike and Hull: "repeated rewarding trials." While Itard felt that his experiment was a failure, educators need to closely observe his teaching procedures. His goals were to develop in Victor socialization, mental training through sensory stimulation, and speech, creating human wants and desires and intelligence.[8] By present standards, these are also recognized as important goals in the teaching of mentally retarded children. Itard's work shows the effectiveness of a system of motivation and rewards, the importance of individualized instruction, and of systematic programming of learning experiences.[9]

Seguin (1812-1880), heir to Itard's observations and experiences, physician, neurologist, and educator, continued the search for training procedures for mental retardation. Instead of working with a single boy like Victor, he established the first public residential facility in France for mentally retarded and devised a curriculum for them.[10] His was a "neurophysiological technique based upon the belief that the impaired nervous systems of retarded could be reeducated by motor and sensory training."[11] In 1846 he published a book outlining the treatment and education of idiots.[12] In his second book, he outlined a residential school program which could be utilized today.[13]

Seguin's philosophy of education is not too different from many of the principles advocated today. He emphasized the education of the whole child, the individualization of instruction, the primary importance of rapport between the teacher and the pupil, the physical comfort of the child during the learning period, and the importance of beginning with the needs of the child, his wants and desires, before progressing into the area of the unknown.[14]

Seguin has made a challenging contribution to the area of mental retardation, and the reader is referred to other of his works for a more extensive research on his relationship to this area of interest.[15]

However, Seguin was not successful in restoring severely

retarded children to normal functioning, and the early hopes of society for the residential school soon faded. At the end of the nineteenth century, a wave of pessimism swept the country. No longer were residential schools viewed as training institutions for the habilitation of the mentally retarded. Instead, they were viewed as custodial facilities for children and adults who were hopelessly dependent. Only in the last decade or so has there been a strong resurgence in training.[16]

Marie Montessori (1870-1956) elaborated still further upon the Itard and Seguin procedures in developing a training program for the mentally retarded in the residential facilities of Rome. Her techniques for the retarded were given less of a trial in the United States than in some countries of Europe and Asia because of the pessimism following Seguin's efforts.

She stressed ten rules of education which she considered equally appropriate for preschool normal and school-age trainable children. These ten rules are:

1. Children are different from adults and need to be approached differently.
2. Learning comes from within and is spontaneous.
3. Children need a childhood environment which stresses free play, games, and colorful materials.
4. Children love order.
5. Children must have freedom of choice.
6. Children love silence.
7. Children prefer work to play.
8. Children love repetition.
9. Children have a sense of personal dignity.
10. Children utilize their environment to improve themselves.[17]

The Montessori method is an approach to education which emphasizes the potential of the child, and which attempts to develop this potential by means of a prepared environment, utilizing specially trained teachers and uniquely designed learning materials and apparatus having an inherent appeal to the preschool or trainable school-age child. Its aim in education is to prepare for a lifetime of learning and to keep abreast in a changing society.[18] Her greatest impact in the United States was in regular kindergarten. Present-day research tends to evidence a resurgence of interest in the Montessori method,[19] an interest manifested in a recent book by Standing on a revolution in education.[20]

To become more aware of her principles and practices, the reader is urged to read her books.[21] An increasing number of journals have carried articles on Montessori, among them are included several which may be of interest to the reader.[22]

Ovide Decroly (1871-1932) found that the methods used successfully with the mentally defective worked equally well with normal children. In his later years he devoted most of his time working with normal children. His student, Alice Descoeudres, reported that Decroly believed that the education of the mentally defective must center around him and his needs.[23] He and his fellow workers developed many educational games and activities designed to correct the defects observed in the mentally handicapped child by cultivating spontaneous attention and leading the child on to working by himself. Many of the games attempted to develop sensory discriminations, as Itard and others had done, and to train the observations of likeness and differences. Decroly emphasized learning on the part of the mentally defective in terms of the child, in other words, the relation of the child to his school, his family, and the society in which he lives. For a more extensive analysis of his method and observation, the reader is referred to three of his works.[24]

Appendix Two

Definition of Mental Retardation

ALTHOUGH MENTAL RETARDATION has been acknowledged in the writings of man for a period of 2,500 years, no single, universally accepted definition has been developed.[1] Hippocrates (460?-357 B.C.) described several forms of mental retardation involving cranial anomalies; Confucius (551-478 B.C.) wrote about man's responsibility for the "weak-minded."[2]

The absence of such a definition reflects upon the highly relative and complex nature of this human phenomenon. Mental retardation, regardless of its cause or form, is determined primarily on the basis of the sociocultural standards of a given society.[3] It is only natural, therefore, that many of the definitions emphasize the sociological aspects of mental retardation.

"The mentally retarded are children and adults who, as a result of inadequately developed intelligence, are significantly impaired in their ability to learn to adapt to the demands of society."[4]

"Mental retardation is a condition which renders the individual unable to compete in ordinary society because of impaired or incomplete mental development."[5]

"Mental deficiency is a state of incomplete mental development of such a kind and degree that the individual is incapable of adapting himself to the normal environment of his fellows in such a way as to maintain existence independently of supervision, control or external support."[6]

Another factor in the complexity of establishing an adequate inclusive definition is the wide range of causes, complicating the very nature of the problem.

> Mental deficiency is a state of social incompetence obtaining at maturity, or likely to obtain at maturity, resulting from developed mental arrest of constitutional origin; the condition is essentially incurable through treatment and unremediable through training except as treatment and training instill habits which superficially or temporarily compensate for the limitations of the person so affected while under favorable circumstances and for more or less limited periods of time.[7]

In Russia, mental retardation is defined not only in terms of characteristics but also of cause.[8]

Still another factor impeding the development of an acceptable definition is that there is no known technique for directly assessing intelligence or intellectual potential.[9] This factor causes the individual's capacity to be inferred on the basis of his performance on such tests as the Stanford-Binet Intelligence Scale or the Wechsler Intelligence Scale for Children. Definitions begin to incorporate the IQ or MA.

In 1910, Goddard considered a child feebleminded if he were more than two years backward on an intelligence test.[10] Doll extended Goddard's concept by indicating that "feeblemindedness is defined psychologically as intellectual retardation of two years at an age below nine or three years at an age above nine."[11]

There has been a great deal of controversy concerning the upper limits of mental deficiency and the IQ was set variously at points from 60[12] to 65[13] and 70[14], up to 80 or 85.[15] Variability of IQ limits from country to country, for special education ranges as follows:

Argentina, Australia, Peru — 50-80
German Federal Republic — 65-85
Switzerland — 70-90
Norway — 50-70.[16]

Generally, the higher the cultural emphasis on academic excellence in the regular grades, the higher the IQ limits for special education.

Research in the area of mental retardation has shown that IQ scores are not accurate as predictions of achievement. There is no definite line of demarcation between educable and trainable mentally retarded children. Similarly, even the expert would have difficulty in making fine-line distinctions. These borderline groups, between the trainable and educable, or between custodial and semidependent, must be answered by criteria other than IQ scores. These criteria often include descriptions of the physical, social, and intellectual capacities of the children concerned. Today there are numerous authorities in the field of mental retardation who desire to abandon completely the use of standardized intelligence tests, for they believe that such tests are too influenced by cultural factors.

"Mental retardation, according to the American Association on Mental Deficiency,* is a group of conditions which result from below average intellectual function."[17] Heber, in his manual for the AAMD, arrived at the following definition: "Mental retardation refers to (1) subaverage general intellectual functioning, (2) which originates during the developmental period, and (3) is associated with impairments in adaptive behavior."[18]

Definitions of mental retardation are developed along numerous lines of interest and inquiry, however, as our knowledge of this problem increases, the definitions of mental retardation will become more precise.

The term *feeblemindedness* was common to American literature until approximately 1945,[19] but today it is rarely used in the United States because of its acquired undesirable connotations. To this point, no term other than *mental retardation* has been introduced; however, the condition of retardation

---

* Hereinafter, reference will be made to this association by the letters AAMD.

also has been identified by Savage as *amentia;* by Segar as *imbecillites;* by Vogel as *Fatuitas ingenii;* by Linnaeus as *morosis;* by Fodere as *demence inee;* by Willis as *stupiditas;* by Pinel as *idiotism;* by some English writers and by Esquirol and the majority of encyclopedias and dictionaries as *idiocy.*[20]

Another label given is *mental deficiency,* a term generally used in a manner synonymous with the AAMD concept of mental retardation. This type of definition, which differentiates retardation from deficiency, frequently appear in psychological and medical literature.[21]

<h3 style="text-align:center">CLASSIFICATION OF MENTAL RETARDATION</h3>

After considerable experience in applying the Binet-Simon Scale to institutionalized patients, Henry Goddard,[22] one of the first to introduce the work of Binet and Simon into this country, recommended a system of classification according to test ratings as follows: *idiots,* those with a mental age up to and including two years; *imbeciles,* those with a mental age of from three to seven years inclusive; *morons,* those with a mental age of from eight to twelve years.[23] These terms are now used infrequently and are nearly extinct. Today, as society becomes more accepting, we prefer to use terms with a more sophisticated connotation.

The AAMD classification of measured intelligence is divided into five categories: borderline, mild, moderate, severe, profound. The boundaries of each division will vary from test to test.

The American Psychiatric Association organizes the subnormal into three groups: mild, moderate, severe. The association considers mild to mean individuals with IQ in the 75 to 85 range, moderate in the 50 to 75 range, and severe in the 0 to 50 range.[24]

The classification established by the American Psychiatric Association, although useful as a frame of reference, does not conform to current practices in the field. This classification tends to lead to oversimplification of something very complex and perplexing. Moreover, within each level there are wide differences of ability and potentiality, and overlapping is considerable between levels. Recognizing these fallacies, the National Association for Retarded Children suggests the following:

> marginal-dependent (educable)
> semi-dependent (trainable)
> dependent (total care).[25]

The educable mentally retarded pupil has been defined as having IQ scores between 50 and 75 and as having, or a prognosis that they will have, learning difficulties in the regular grades.[26] Children who are classified as trainable have been defined as having IQs from about 30 or 35 to 50 or 55. This means that they develop intellectually at about one-third to one-half the rate of the average child.[27] Custodial, or nursing, mentally defective children, are those who are almost totally dependent, with IQs up to 30. These then, the subnormal, below-average individuals are termed mentally retarded, mentally deficient, mentally handicapped or intellectually limited.

Education of the trainable mentally retarded dates back to 1801 when Itard published his study on the Wild Boy of Aveyron. Social action for the problem began prior to 1850 when both Americans and Europeans opened special schools; however, not until 1900 did teachers differentiate between or separate the severely and moderately retarded. When differentiation did occur, the lower educable limit reached to an IQ of 30.

These graduations eventually came to be closely related with the "educability" concept. This dictum evolved: "The idiot never learns to talk, the imbecile never learns to read, the moron never learns to think."[28] Through this reasoning, a distinction gradually arose between "educable" and "uneducable."

Since 1950 new opportunities have opened for the growth of educational studies for trainable mentally retarded persons.[29] The presently widespread opportunities for the trainable mentally retarded began largely under the stimulation of parent groups and interested professional personnel.[30] A substantial body of literature has now been developed, which is presented by Harold M. Williams and J. E. Wallace in the form of a bibliographical review.[31]

As has been noted, many definitions of mental retardation and its various degrees have been reported. Some authors attempt a composite definition; others have offered definitions from various points of view: education, psychology, sociology and medicine. However, retardation must be studied from a composite of all of these disciplines.

Persons classified as trainable have already been defined as having IQs from 30 or 35 to 50 or 55. The trainable person is limited in terms of academic skills, so his usual training program stresses help primarily in self-care, social habits, and adjustment to his environment.

In drafting legislation, certain guidelines have been established in state laws regarding the nature of the group to be served through a school program. "Among the bases for these guidelines are: "(1) a certain IQ range, based on adequately administered intelligence tests; (2) the fact that a child has been declared ineligible for regular grades or 'educable' classes; and (3) a description term such as 'trainable.' "[32]

Educators are also concerned with medical classifications for the information needed in providing special class groupings and in solving educational problems.

Successful Ministry to the Retarded

Classification of Trainable Mentally Retarded Children

CAUSE OF RETARDATION	PERCENTAGE OF TOTAL TMR
Organic Brain Injury	37.15
Mongolism	33.05
Undifferentiated and Unknown	26.94
Cretinism	1.22
Cultural-Familial	0.82
Microcephaly	0.41
Other	0.41

SOURCE: J. V. Hottel, *The Tennessee Experimental Program of Classes for Severely Mentally Retarded Children: Interim Report of the Study,* p. 134.

Some states must themselves determine the level at which a person is called severely or only moderately retarded. The term *trainable* is used by Minnesota[33] and North Carolina.[34] The California statutes determine the definition in terms of social competence.[35] Some states use the criterion of ineligibility for upper-range special classes.*

---

* California, Illinois, and New Jersey adhere to this method of ascertaining who is the severely retarded person.

Notes

INTRODUCTION

1. Julia S. Molloy, *Trainable Children,* p. 1.

CHAPTER 1

1. L. A. Kanner, *Miniature Textbook of Feeblemindedness,* p. 8.
2. Lawson Lowrey, "The Relationship of Feeblemindedness to Behavior Disorders," pp. 96-100.
3. "Fact Sheet on Mental Retardation," Illinois Council for Mentally Retarded Children.
4. C. B. Davenport and F. H. Danielson, *The Hill Folk* (report publ. 1913).
5. Stanley P. Davies, *The Mentally Retarded in Society,* p. 87.
6. "Fact Sheet on Mental Retardation."
7. Ibid.
8. Cyrus W. Stimson, "Understanding the Mongoloid Child," pp. 56-59.
9. Ibid.
10. Ibid.
11. "Fact Sheet on Mental Retardation."
12. Samuel Livingston, *Living with Epileptic Seizures,* p. 3.
13. Ibid., pp. 37-39.
14. Ibid., p. 82.

CHAPTER 2

1. Harold M. Williams and J. E. Wallace, *Education of the Severely Retarded Child: A Bibliographical Review,* p. 18.
2. Lawson Lowrey, "The Relationship of Feeblemindedness to Behavior Disorders," pp. 96-100.
3. Alfred Baumeister, *Mental Retardation,* p. 86.
4. Ibid.
5. Bernice B. Baumgartner, *Helping the Trainable Mentally Retarded Child,* p. 18. Reprinted by permission of the publisher (New York: Teachers College Press, 1967; copyright 1967 by Teachers College, Columbia University).
6. Ibid.
7. Baumeister, p. 86.
8. John W. Howe and Thomas W. Smith, "Characteristics of Mentally Retarded Children," p. 32.
9. Lloyd Dunn, ed., *Exceptional Children in the Schools,* p. 141; and Harry J. Baker, *Introduction to Exceptional Children,* p. 261.
10. William Cruickshank and Orville Johnson, *Education of Exceptional Children and Youth,* pp. 239-40.
11. R. L. Cromwell, "Selected Aspects of Personality Development in Mentally Retarded Children," pp. 44-51, as cited by Max L. Hutt and Robert Gibby, *The Mentally Retarded Child,* p. 202.
12. Baumgartner, p. 56.
13. Ibid., p. 18.
14. M. Woodward, "Early Experience and Behavior Disorders in Severely Subnormal Children," pp. 174-84.
15. Ignacy Goldberg, "Some Aspects of the Current Status of Education and Training in the United States for Trainable Mentally Retarded Children," pp. 146-54, citing Williams and Wallace, p. 11.
16. Natalie Perry, *Teaching the Mentally Retarded Child,* p. 71.
17. Jerome Rothstein, ed., *Mental Retardation,* p. 60.
18. Baumgartner, *Guiding the Retarded Child,* p. 139.

19. *The Retarded Child Goes to School,* p. 10.
20. LaDonna Bogardus, *Christian Education for Retarded Children and Youth.* pp. 60-62; and Williams and Wallace, p. 17.
21. Ibid.

CHAPTER 3

1. A. W. Melton, "Learning" in *Encyclopedia of Educational Research,* as cited by Jerome Rothstein, ed., *Mental Retardation,* p. 136.
2. Alfred E. Baumeister, ed., *Mental Retardation,* p. 185.
3. Ibid., p. 189.
4. Ibid., p. 191.
5. Jerome Rothstein, *Mental Retardation,* p. 347.
6. William Cruickshank and Orville Johnson, *Education of Exceptional Children and Youth,* pp. 14-15.
7. Baumeister, p. 182.
8. Ibid., p. 104.

CHAPTER 4

1. Martin Luther, *Colloquia Mensalia,* p. 387, as cited by Leo Kanner, *A History of the Care and Study of the Mentally Retarded,* p. 7.
2. Emil Brunner, *The Christian Doctrine of Creation and Redemption,* p. 57.
3. This view is sometimes upheld by parents who have considered their child very special, feeling that he is teaching them many "lessons." This approach has been taken by Dale Evans Rogers in her book *Angel Unaware* and by Edna Schultz, *They Said Kathy Was Retarded.*
4. Edward Seguin, *Idiocy and Its Treatment by the Physiological Method,* p. 47.
5. Sister Mary Theodore, *The Challenge of the Retarded Child,* p. 143.
6. Harold Stubblefield, *The Church's Ministry in Mental Retardation,* p. 57.
7. Ibid.
8. Ibid., p. 56.
9. Ibid., p. 57.
10. Ibid., p. 153.
11. LaDonna Bogardus, *Christian Education for Retarded Children and Youth;* Charles E. Palmer, *The Church and the Exceptional Person;* Charles Kemp, *The Church: The Gifted and the Retarded Child;* Marion O. Lerrigo, *The Mentally Retarded and the Church;* Sigurd D. Peterson, *Retarded Children: God's Children;* G. L. Doll, "Church and the Handicapped Child"; F. E. Henry and C. E. Kemp, "Religion in the Life of the Mentally Retarded"; J. D. Rozeboom, "The Church and 'Exceptional' Children"; Ruth Strang, "What the Pastor Should Know About Special Education."
12. Oliver Graebner, "God Concepts of Mentally Retarded by Picture Projection, pp. 2-3.
13. Ibid.
14. Stubblefield, pp. 58-59.

CHAPTER 5

1. Elmer Towns, "Day School for Retarded and Disturbed Children Is New Ministry," p. 62.
2. Harold W. Stubblefield, *The Church's Ministry in Mental Retardation,* p. 83.
3. Ibid.
4. Ibid., p. 86.
5. Bernice Carlson and David Ginglend, *Play Activities for the Retarded Child,* pp. 15-18; and LaDonna Bogardus, *Christian Education for Retarded Children and Youth,* pp. 15-18.

6. William Cruickshank and Orville Johnson, *Education of Exceptional Children and Youth,* p. 14.
7. Alfred E. Baumeister, ed., *Mental Retardation,* p. 294.
8. Ibid., p. 275.
9. Cruickshank and Johnson, p. 47.
10. Margaret Hudson, *Identification and Evaluation Methods for Teaching Severely Retarded Children,* p. 272.
11. Cruickshank and Johnson, p. 162.
12. Ibid., p. 425.
13. Natalie Perry, *Teaching the Mentally Retarded Child,* p. 32.
14. Ibid.
15. J. Edward Hakes, ed., *An Introduction to Evangelical Christian Education,* p. 154. This author is speaking of the primary department, but the information is extremely relevant to the needs of the mentally retarded.
16. Philip N. Nelbach, "Modern Performance Standards for School Heating and Ventilation," pp. 37-39.
17. Cruickshank and Johnson, p. 16.
18. Ibid., p. 14.
19. Ibid., p. 16.

CHAPTER 6

1. Walter B. Barbe and Edward S. Frierson, eds., *Educating Children with Learning Disabilities,* p. 337.
2. Ibid.
3. Ibid., p. 63.
4. LaDonna Bogardus, *Christian Education for Retarded Children and Youth,* p. 99.
5. Bernice Baumgartner, *Helping the Trainable Mentally Retarded Child,* pp. 59-60.
6. Barbe and Frierson, p. 10.
7. Andrew Wood, *A Manual for Reaching Retarded Children for Christ,* p. 10.
8. Bogardus, p. 100.
9. Alfred E. Baumeister, ed., *Mental Retardation,* p. 128.
10. Natalie Perry, *Teaching the Mentally Retarded Child,* p. 141.
11. Ibid., p. 12.
12. Barbe and Frierson, pp. 141-42.
13. C. S. Lewis, *Letters to Malcolm,* p. 35.
14. Marion J. Erickson, *The Mentally Retarded Child in the Classroom,* p. 66.
15. Ibid., p. 74.
16. One resource book for the teacher is *Helping the Retarded to Know God* by H. Hahn and W. Raasch. The textbook and the instructor's guide are each $1.95. A course to meet the need for qualified teachers for the mentally retarded, it supplies insights into the characteristics and spiritual needs of the retarded, giving the reader basic understanding and skills so he can minister effectively to this much-neglected group.
17. Baumeister, p. 294.
18. Samuel A. Kirk, *Public School Provisions for Severely Retarded,* p. 10.
19. Baumeister, p. 284.

CHAPTER 7

1. LaDonna Bogardus, *Christian Education for Retarded Children and Youth,* p. 68.
2. J. Edward Hakes, *An Introduction to Evangelical Christian Education,* p. 71.

3. Ruth Strang, *Helping Your Child Develop His Potentialities*, p. 83.
4. Marie Egg, *Educating the Child Who Is Different*, p. 84.
5. Strang, p. 83.
6. William Abraham. *A Guide for the Study of Exceptional Children*, p. 69.
7. Bogardus, p. 78.
8. Ibid.
9. Ethel Barrett, *Storytelling — It's Easy*, pp. 54-60. This is an excellent book on basic, practical principles of storytelling, and it is very useful for the church school teacher. Its methods are applicable to the trainable mentally retarded.
10. Isabel B. Burger, *Creative Play Acting*, p. 12. Although this book is not designed for the play needs of trainable retardates, much of its material can be utilized by the teacher in working with the severely retarded.
11. Burger, p. 25.
12. Bernice Carlson and David Ginglend, *Play Activities for the Retarded Child*, p. 29.
13. Alan Klein, *Role Playing*, p. 71.
14. G. J. Meyers, *Puppets Can Teach, Too* (Minneapolis: Augsburg, n.d.) is a good book on puppetry. It may be ordered from Concordia Publishing House. Paperback copies are $3.50.
15. The substance of this material concerning the use of puppetry is taken from the article by Frances Koenig, "Implications in the Use of Puppetry with Handicapped Children," pp. 111-12.
16. Catharine Williams, *Learning from Pictures*, p. 1.
17. Ibid., pp. 18-22.
18. Louis Rosenzweig and Julia Long, *Understanding and Teaching the Dependent Retarded Child*, p. 164.
19. Julia Molloy, *Trainable Children*, p. 3.
20. Natalie Perry, *Teaching the Mentally Retarded Child*, pp. 159-61.
21. Ibid., p. 93.
22. William Cruickshank and Frederick Ratzeburg, *A Teaching Method for Brain-Injured and Hyperactive Children*, p. 182.
23. Molloy, p. 334.
24. Cruickshank and Ratzeburg, p. 185.
25. Perry, pp. 93-94.
26. Andrew Wood, *A Manual for Reaching Retarded Children for Christ*, p. 17.
27. Books for rhythm bands include Ida S. Krawitz, *How to Teach Rhythms and Rhythm Bands* (New York: G. Schirmer, 1955); and Susanna B. Saffran, *First Book of Creative Rhythms* (New York: Holt, Rinehart, & Winston, 1963).

CHAPTER 8

1. Abraham Levinson, *The Mentally Retarded Child*, p. 21.
2. Laura L. Dittmann, *The Mentally Retarded Child at Home*, p. 3.
3. Ibid.
4. Stanley C. Mahoney, "Observations Concerning Counseling with Parents of Mentally Retarded Children," p. 84.
5. Ida Rappaport, "Parents and Retarded Children," p. 182.
6. David Melton, *Todd*, p. x.
7. LaDonna Bogardus, *Christian Education for Retarded Children and Youth*, p. 19.
8. Irving Bisler, "Psychopathology and Other Adjustments with the Mentally Retarded" as cited by Alfred A. Baumeister, ed., *Mental Retardation*, p. 136.
9. Charles E. Palmer, *The Church and the Exceptional Person*, p. 136.
10. Bogardus, p. 19.

11. Palmer, p. 26. Used by permission of Abingdon Press.
12. Levinson, p. 29.
13. Ibid., p. 30.
14. Melton, p. 16.
15. Information is available at local public aid offices in that state. The legislation code number is HB 2783.
16. Levinson, p. 36.
17. Mahoney, p. 82.
18. Levinson, p. 39.

CHAPTER 9

1. Sister Mary Theodore, *The Retarded Child in Touch with God*, p. 8.
2. Thomas E. Jordan, *The Mentally Retarded*, p. 341.
3. W. Wolfensberger and R. Kurtz, eds., *Management of the Family of the Mentally Retarded*, p. 355.
4. Ibid., pp. 355-56.
5. Edward S. Golden, "Pastoral Counselling and Guidance with the Mental Retardate," p. 34.
6. Charles F. Kemp, *The Church: The Gifted and the Retarded Child*, p. 159.
7. Ibid., p. 159.
8. *Psychology Today*, p. 497.
9. Jane Warters, *Group Guidance*, p. 217.
10. Golden, p. 35.
11. Charles E. Palmer, pp. 25-26.
12. Laura L. Dittmann, *The Mentally Retarded Child at Home*, p. 6.
13. Kemp, p. 155.

APPENDIX ONE

1. Lloyd M. Dunn, ed., *Exceptional Children in the Schools*, p. 142. Used by permission of Holt, Rinehart and Winston, Inc.
2. "Nicholas, Saint," *Encyclopedia Americana*, 20:322.
3. Dunn, p. 142.
4. Samuel Kirk and Orville Johnson, *Educating the Retarded Child*, p. 70.
5. Ibid., p. 76.
6. Edward Seguin, *Idiocy and Its Treatment by the Physiological Method*, pp. 17-18.
7. Ibid.
8. Kirk and Johnson, pp. 71-73.
9. Dunn, p. 143.
10. Ibid.
11. Ibid.
12. Sequin, *Traitment Moral, Hygiene et Education des Idiots.*
13. Sequin, *Idiocy and Its Treatment . . .* , pp. 172-202.
14. Kirk and Johnson, p. 78.
15. Seguin, *New Facts and Remarks Concerning Idiocy*, a lecture delivered before the New York Medical Journal Assn. (Oct. 15, 1869); *Résumé de ce que nous avons fait pendent quatorze mois; Hygiene et Education; Images Graduees a l'usage des Enfants Arrieres et Idiots.*
16. Dunn, pp. 145-46.
17. Ibid., p. 146.
18. Urban Fleege, "Developing Your Child's Potential Through the Montessori Method," lecture given Aug. 15, 1967.
19. Fleege, "Marie Montessori," *New Catholic Encyclopedia* 9:1090-91.
20. Mortimer E. Standing, *The Montessori Revolution in Education.*
21. Marie Montessori, *The Montessori Method; Education for a New World; Formation of Man; Spontaneous Activity in Education*, vol. 1; *The Absorbent*

Mind; Dorothy Canfield Fisher, *Montessori for Parents.*

22. "How to Start a Montessori School," *New City* (Apr. 15, 1962); "Montessori in Your Home," *Ave Maria* (Feb. 9, 1963); "Teaching 3-Year-Olds: A Revival of Montessori," *The Sign* (May 1963); "Montessori, A Revival in Full Swing," *United States Catholic* (Dec. 1964); "Montessori: Education Begins at Three," *Look* (Jan. 26, 1965); "The Promise of Montessori," *Extension* magazine (Jan. 1966).

23. Alice Descoeudres, *The Education of Mentally Defective Children.*

24. Ovid. Decroly, *La Classification des enfants anormaux; L'initiation a l'activite intellectualle et motrice par les jeux educatifs;* and *La Pratique des tests mentaux.*

APPENDIX TWO

1. R. C. Scheerenberger, *Mental Retardation Abstracts,* p. 432.
2. Ibid.
3. Ibid.
4. "A Proposed Program for National Action to Combat Mental Retardation," p. 1.
5. E. French and C. Scott, *Child in the Shadows,* p. 40.
6. A. F. Tredgold, *A Textbook of Mental Deficiency,* p. 4.
7. E. A. Doll, "The Essentials of an Inclusive Concept of Mental Deficiency," p. 217.
8. Scheerenberger, p. 432.
9. Ibid.
10. Ibid., p. 433.
11. J. Wallin, *Children with Mental and Physical Handicaps,* p. 17.
12. R. Pintner, *The Feebleminded Child.*
13. D. Wechsler, *Measurement of Adult Intelligence.*
14. M. A. Merrill, "Significance of the IQ's on the Revised Stanford-Binet Scales," pp. 641-51.
15. Wallin, pp. 17-29.
16. UNESCO, *Organization of Special Education for Mentally Deficient,* cited by Lloyd N. Dunn, ed.; *Exceptional Children in the Schools,* p. 73.
17. J. Willard Agee, "The Minister Looks at Mental Retardation," pp. 12-22.
18. R. F. Heber, "A Manual on Terminology and Classification in Mental Retardation," pp. 499-500, as cited by Dunn, p. 54.
19. Scheerenberger, p. 434.
20. Edward Seguin, *Idiocy and Its Treatment by the Physiological Method,* p. 29.
21. Scheerenberger, p. 434.
22. Henry Goddard, "Feeblemindedness: A Question of Definition," p. 220.
23. Goddard, *Feeble-Mindedness, Its Course and Consequences,* p. 15.
24. Louis Rosenzweig and Julia Long, *Understanding and Teaching the Retarded Child,* p. 12.
25. Ibid., p. 13.
26. Dunn, p. 71.
27. Ibid., p. 130.
28. Jerome H. Rothstein, ed., *Mental Retardation,* p. 335.
29. Harold M. Williams, *Education of the Severely Retarded Child,* p. 3.
30. Ibid.
31. Harold M. Williams and J. E. Wallace, *Education of the Severely Retarded Child: A Bibliographical Review.*
32. Williams, p. 5.
33. Minnesota, *Statutes, Annotated* (1959).
34. North Carolina, *Statutes* (1957).
35. Williams, p. 5.

Bibliography

Abraham, Willard. *A Guide for the Study of Exceptional Children.* Boston: Sargent, 1956.

—————. *The Slow Learner.* New York: Ctr. for Applied Res. in Ed., 1964.

Agee, J. Willard. "Lest the Least Be Lost: Character Education of the Retarded." *American Journal of Mental Deficiency* 58 (Nov. 1958):290-94.

—————. "The Minister Looks at Mental Retardation." *Pastoral Psychology* 13 (Sept. 1962):12-22.

Baker, Harry J. *Introduction to Exceptional Children.* New York: Macmillan, 1959.

Barbe, Walter B. *The Exceptional Child.* Washington, D.C.: Ctr. for Applied Res. in Ed., 1963.

Barbe, Walter B., and Frierson, Edward S., eds. *Educating Children with Learning Disabilities.* New York: Appleton-Century-Crofts, 1967.

Barrett, Ethel. *Storytelling — It's Easy.* Los Angeles: Cowman, 1960.

Bauer, Charles E. *Retarded Children Are People.* Milwaukee: Bruce, 1964.

Baumeister, Alfred E., ed. *Mental Retardation.* Chicago: Aldine, 1967.

Baumgartner, Bernice B. *Guiding the Retarded Child.* New York: Day, 1965.

—————. *Helping the Trainable Mentally Retarded Child.* New York: Teachers College, Columbia U., 1967.

Bogardus, LaDonna. *Christian Education for Retarded Children and Youth.* New York: Abingdon, 1963.

Bowers, Mabel. "Music as a Means of Increasing Responsiveness in Young Mental Defectives." *Journal of Exceptional Children* 3 (Feb. 1937):95-96.

Brunner, Emil. *The Christian Doctrine of Creation and Redemption.* Trans. Olive Wyon. Philadelphia: Westminster, 1952.

Buck, Pearl S. *The Child Who Never Grew.* New York: Day, 1950.

——————. *The Gifts They Bring.* New York: Day, 1965.

Burger, Isabel B. *Creative Play Acting.* New York: Ronald, 1966.

Byrne, May E. "Curriculum Planning for Exceptional Children." *Journal of Exceptional Children* 12 (May 1946):231-34.

Carlson, Bernice W. *Act It Out.* Nashville: Abingdon, 1956.

——————. *Make It Yourself.* Nashville: Abingdon, 1958.

Carlson, Bernice W., and Ginglend, David R. *Play Activities for the Retarded Child.* New York: Abingdon, 1961.

——————. *Recreation for Retarded Teenagers and Young Adults.* Nashville: Abingdon, 1968.

Condell, James F. "Parental Attitudes Toward Mental Retardation." *American Journal of Mental Deficiency* 71 (1966): 85-92.

Creative Ways of Teaching the Mentally Handicapped. Honolulu: Dept. of Ed., Special Services Branch, 1966.

Cromwell, R. L. "Selected Aspects of Personality Development in Mentally Retarded Children." *Exceptional Children* 28 (1961):44-51.

Cruikshank, William M., ed. *Psychology of Exceptional Children and Youth.* Englewood Cliffs, N.J.: Prentice-Hall, 1963.

Cruikshank, William M., and Johnson, Orville. *Education of Exceptional Children and Youth.* Englewood Cliffs, N.Y.: Prentice-Hall, 1958.

Cruikshank, William M. et al. *A Teaching Method for Brain-Injured and Hyperactive Children.* New York: Syracuse U., 1961.

Davies, Stanley P., and Ecob, Katherine G. *The Mentally Retarded in Society.* New York: Columbia U., 1959.

Decroly, Ovid. *La Classification des enfants anormaux.* Grand Imp. A. Vander Haeghen, 1906.

——————. *L'initiation a l'actifite intellectualle et motrice par les jeux aducatifs.* Neuchatel Delachaux and Niestle, 1914.

————. *La Pratique des tests mentaux.* Paris: Alcan, 1928.

Descoeudres, Alice. *The Education of Mentally Defective Children.* Trans. Ernest F. Row. Boston: Heath, 1928.

DeHaan, Robert F., and Kough, Jack. *Identifying Children with Special Needs.* Chicago: Science Res. Assoc., 1956.

Dittman, Laura L. *The Mentally Retarded Child at Home: A Manual for Parents.* Children's Bur. Pub. No. 374. Washington, D.C.: Gov't. Printing Office, 1958.

Doll, E. A. "The Essentials of an Inclusive Concept of Mental Deficiency." *American Journal of Mental Deficiency* 46 (1941):217.

Doll, G. L. "Church and the Handicapped Child." *Christianity Today* 9 (Feb. 26, 1965):15-19.

Dunn, Lloyd M., ed. *Exceptional Children in the Schools.* New York: Holt, Rinehart, & Winston, 1963.

Dunn, Lloyd M., and Baker, Harry J. *Introduction to Exceptional Children.* New York: Macmillan, 1953.

Dybwad, Gunnar. "Not All of One Mold." *International Journal of Religious Education* 37 (May 1961):16-17.

Ebersole, Eleanor. *Christian Education for Socially Handicapped Children and Youth.* Philadelphia: United Church, 1964.

Ecob, Katherine G. *Deciding What's Best for Your Retarded Child.* New York: State Soc. for Mental Health, 1955.

Egg, Marie. *Educating the Child Who Is Different.* New York: Day, 1968.

————. *When a Child Is Different.* New York: Day, 1960.

Ehlers, Walter H. *Mothers of Retarded Children: How They Feel, Where They Find Help.* Springfield, Ill.: Thomas, 1966.

Erickson, Marion J. *The Mentally Retarded Child in the Classroom.* New York: Macmillan, 1967.

"Fact Sheet on Mental Retardation." Illinois Council for Mentally Retarded Children, 1966.

Fisher, Dorothy C. *Montessori for Parents.* Cambridge, Mass.: Bentley, 1965.

Fitzibbon, Walter C. "A Rationale for Crafts for the Educable Mentally Retarded." *Exceptional Children* 32 (1965): 243-46.

Fleege, Urban. "Developing Your Child's Potential Through the Montessori Method." Lecture, Lake Forest College, Ill. (Aug. 15, 1967).

—————. "Marie Montessori." In *New Catholic Encyclopedia*, vol. 9. New York: McGraw-Hill, 1967.

Fletcher, H. J., and Deckter, Jack. *Puppet Book*. New York: Greenberg, 1947.

French, Edward L., and Scott, J. Clifford. *Child in the Shadows: A Manual for Parents of Retarded Children*. New York, Lippincott, 1960.

Goddard, Henry. "Feeblemindedness: A Question of Definition." *Journal of Psychlo-Aesthetics* 12 (1911):220.

—————. *Feeble-Mindedness, Its Course and Consequences*. New York: Macmillan, 1914.

Goldberg, Ignacy. "Some Aspects of the Current Status of Education and Training in the United States for Trainable Mentally Retarded Children." *Exceptional Children* 23 (Dec. 1957):146-54.

Golden, Edward S. "Pastoral Counseling and Guidance with the Mental Retardate." *Pastoral Psychology* 13 (Sept. 1962):31-36.

Graebner, Oliver. "God Concepts of Mentally Retarded by Picture Projection." *The Star* 4 (Fall, 1966):2-3.

Hafemeister, N. R. "Development of Curriculum for the Trainable Child." *American Journal of Mental Deficiency* 55 (April 1951):495-501.

Hahn, Hans R., and Raasch, Werner H. *Instructors Guide for Helping the Retarded to Know God*. St. Louis, Mo.: Concordia, 1969.

Heath, Earl J. "Field Trips for Life Experiences." *Mental Retardation* 4 (1966):42-43.

Heber, R. F. "A Manual on Terminology and Classification in Mental Retardation." *American Journal of Mental Deficiency* 65 (1961):499-500.

Henry, F. E., and Kemp, C. E. "Religion in the Life of the Mentally Retarded." *Journal of Religion and Health* 4 (Oct. 1964):59-65.

Hottel, J. V. *The Tennessee Experimental Program of Day Classes for Severely Mentally Retarded Children: Interim Report of the Study.* Nashville, Peabody College, 1956.

Howe, C. E. "A Comparison of Motor Skills of Mentally Retarded and Normal Children." *American Journal of Mental Deficiency* 25 (1959):352-54.

Howe, John W., and Smith, Thomas W. "Characteristics of Mentally Retarded Children." Bulletin No. 3. Los Angeles: Cty. Supt. of Schools, L.A. Brd. of Ed., 1950.

Hudson, Margaret. *Identification and Evaluation Methods for Teaching Severely Retarded Children.* Nashville: Peabody College, 1959.

Hutt, Max L., and Gibby, Robert G. *The Mentally Retarded Child.* Rockleigh, N.J.: Allyn & Bacon, 1958.

An Introduction to a Program of Christian Education for the Religious Instruction of Mentally Retarded Children. Vermont Assoc. for Retarded Children, 1961.

Isern, Betty. "Music in Special Education." *Journal of Music Therapy* 1 (1964):139-42.

Jacobs, Frances. *Finger Plays and Action Rhymes.* New York: Lothrop, Lee, & Shepard, 1941.

Jolly, Donald M., and Nelson, Charles. *Religious Education — A Manual for Volunteer Teachers.* Butlerville, Ind.: Muscataville State School, 1960.

Jordan, Thomas E. *The Mentally Retarded.* Columbus, Ohio: Merrill, 1961.

Kanner, Leo A. "Feeblemindedness, Absolute, Relative and Apparent." *Nervous Children* 7 (1948):365-97.

————. *A History of the Care and Study of the Mentally Retarded.* Springfield, Ill.: Thomas, 1964.

————. *Miniature Textbook of Feeblemindedness.* New York: Child Care Pubns., 1949.

Kemp, Charles. *The Church: The Gifted and the Retarded Child.* St. Louis: Bethany, 1957.

Kirk, Samuel A. *Public School Provisions for Severely Retarded.* Albany: N.Y. State Interdptl. Health Resources Bd., 1957.

Klein, Alan. *Role Playing.* New York: Association, 1956.

Knight, D.; Ludwig, A. J.; and Pope, L. "The Role of Varied Therapies in the Rehabilitation of the Retarded Child." *American Journal of Mental Deficiency* 61 (1957):508-15.

Koenig, Frances. "Implications in the Use of Puppetry with Handicapped Children." *Journal of Exceptional Children* 17 (Jan. 1961):111-12.

Krause, Irl Brown. *Religious Education for Mentally Retarded Children.* Memphis, Tenn.: Memphis State U., 1961.

Lerrigo, Marion O. *The Mentally Retarded and the Church.* New York: Nat. Council of Churches, 1959.

Levinson, Abraham. *The Mentally Retarded Child.* New York: Day, 1952.

Lewis, C. S. *Letters to Malcolm.* New York: Harcourt, Brace, & World, 1964.

Lister, Rebecca. *Jewish Religious Education for the Retarded Child.* New York: Union of Amer. Heb. Cong., 1959.

Livingston, Samuel. *Living with Epileptic Seizures.* Springfield, Ill.: Thomas, 1963.

Lowrey, Lawson. "Relationship of Feeblemindedness to Behavior Problems." *Journal of Psycho-Asthenics* 33:96-100.

Luther, Martin. *Colloquia Mensalia.* London: Du-Gard, 1952.

Mahoney, Stanley C. "Observations Concerning Counseling with Parents of Mentally Retarded Children." *American Journal of Mental Deficiency,* July 1958, pp. 81-86.

Matson, Virginia F. "A Neglected Ministry: What of the Handicapped Child?" *Christianity Today* 5 (Jan. 1961):343-45.

Melton, A. W. "Learning." In *Encyclopedia of Educational Research.* New York: Macmillan, 1941.

Melton, David. *Todd.* New York: Dell, 1968.

Merrill, M. A. "Significance of the IQs on the Revised Stanford-Binet Scales." *Journal of Educational Psychology,* 1964, pp. 641-51.

Molloy, Julia S. *Teaching the Retarded Child to Talk.* New York: Day, 1961.

————. *Trainable Children.* New York: Day, 1963.

Montessori, Marie. *The Absorbent Mind.* New York: Holt, 1967.

————. *Activity in Education.* Vol. 1. Cambridge, Mass.: Bentley, 1965.

————. *Education for a New World*. Wheaton: Theosophical, 1959.

————. *Formation of Man*. Wheaton: Theosophical, 1962.

————. *The Montessori Method*. Philadelphia: Stokes, 1912.

————. *Spontaneous Activity in Education*. Vol. 1. Cambridge, Mass.: Bentley, 1965.

Nelbach, Philip N. "Modern Performance Standards for School Heating and Ventilation." *American Journal of Public Health* 112 (Jan. 1946):37-39.

"Nicholas, Saint." In *Encyclopedia Americana*, vol. 20. New York: Grolier, 1962.

Palmer, Charles E. *The Church and the Exceptional Person*.

Perry, Natalie. *Teaching the Mentally Retarded Child*. New York: Columbia U., 1960.

Peterson, S. "Pastoral Care of Parents of Mentally Retarded Persons." *Pastoral Psychology* 13 (Sept. 1962):37-44.

Peterson, Sigurd D. *Retarded Children: God's Children*. Philadelphia: Westminster, 1960.

Pintner, R. *The Feebleminded Child*. 2d ed. Worcester, Mass.: Clark U., 1933.

A Program of Christian Education for Use with Mentally Retarded Children. Vermont Assoc. for Retarded Children, 1961.

"A Proposed Program for National Action to Combat Mental Retardation." In *President's Panel on Mental Retardation*. Washington, D.C.: Gov't. Printing Office, 1962.

Providing a Program of Christian Education for Mentally Retarded. The Lutheran Church, Missouri Synod, 1961.

Psychology Today: An Introduction. Del Mar., Calif.: Communications Res. Machines, 1970.

The Retarded Child Goes to School. Public Affairs Pamphlet No. 349. Washington, D.C.

Robins, Ferris, and Robins, Jennet. *Educational Rhythmics for Mentally and Physically Handicapped Children*. New York: Association, 1968.

Rogers, Dale Evans. *Angel Unaware*. New Jersey: Revell, 1953.

Rosenzweig, Louis, and Long, Julia. *Understanding and Teaching the Dependent Retarded Child.* Darien, Conn.: Educational Publ., 1960.

Rothstein, Jerome H., ed. *Mental Retardation.* New York: Holt, Rinehart, & Winston, 1964.

Rozeboom, J.D. "The Church and 'Exceptional' Children." *International Journal of Religious Education* 30 (July-Aug. 1957):15-16.

Schattner, Regina. *Creative Dramatics for Handicapped Children.* New York: Day, 1967.

Scheerenberger, R. C. *Mental Retardation Abstracts.* Vol. 1. No. 4. Washington, D.C.: Gov't. Printing Office, 1964.

Schultz, Edna. *They Said Kathy Was Retarded.* Chicago: Moody, 1963.

Seguin, Edward. *Hygiene et Education.* Paris, 1843.

————. *Idiocy and Its Treatment by the Physiological Method.* New York: Columbia U., 1907.

————. *Images Graduees a l'usage des Enfants Arrieres et Idiots.* Paris, 1846.

————. *New Facts and Remarks Concerning Idiocy.* New York: Wood, 1870.

————. *Résumé de ce que nous avons fait pendent quatorze mois.* Paris, 1839.

————. *Traitment Moral, Hygiene et Education des Idiots.* Paris, 1846.

Snodgrass, Joel. "Mental Retardation and Religion." *Mental Retardation Abstracts* 3 (Oct.-Dec. 1966):502-8. An annotated bibliography.

Slaughter, Stella. *The Mentally Retarded Child and His Parent.* Illinois: Harper, 1960.

Stair, Ernest R. "Religion and the Handicapped Child." *Religious Education* 62(1968):352-54.

Standing, Mortimer E. *The Montessori Revolution in Education.* New York: Schocken Books, 1966.

Stimson, Cyrus W. "Understanding the Mongoloid Child." *Today's Health* 46 (Nov. 1968):56-59.

Strang, Ruth. *Helping Your Child Develop His Potentialities.* New York: Dutton, 1965.

————. "What the Pastor Should Know About Special Education." *Pastoral Psychology* 15 (Mar. 1964):19-23.

Stubblefield, Harold W. *The Church's Ministry in Mental Retardation.* Nashville: Broadman, 1965.

————. "The Ministry and Mental Retardation." *Journal of Religion and Health,* January, 1964, pp. 136-47.

Talbot, G. "Sunday School for the Mentally Retarded." *Moody Monthly* 67 (Dec. 1966):44-47.

Theodore, Sister Mary. *The Challenge of the Retarded Child.* Milwaukee: Bruce, 1959.

————. *The Retarded Child in Touch with God.* Boston: Daughters of St. Paul, 1966.

Thomas, Janet K. *How to Teach and Administer Classes for Mentally Retarded Children.* Minneapolis, Minn.: Denison, 1968.

Towns, Elmer. "Day School for Retarded and Disturbed Children Is New Ministry." *Christian Life,* October, 1969, p. 62.

Tredgold, A. F. *A Textbook of Mental Deficiency.* 6th ed. Baltimore: Wood, 1937.

UNESCO. *Organization of Special Education for Mentally Deficient Children.* Geneva: Internat. Bur. of Ed., 1960.

Wallin, J. *Children with Mental and Physical Handicaps.* New York: Prentice-Hall, 1949.

Warters, Jane. *Group Guidance.* New York: McGraw-Hill, 1960.

Wechsler, D. *Measurement of Adult Intelligence.* 2d ed. Baltimore: Wood, 1941.

Williams, Catharine. *Learning from Pictures.* Washington, D.C.: Dept. AV Instr., 1963.

Williams, Harold M. *Education of the Severely Retarded Child.* Bulletin No. 20. Washington, D.C.: US Dept. HEW, 1961.

Williams, Harold M., and Wallace, J. E. *Education of the Severely Retarded Child: A Bibliographical Review.* Bulletin No. 12. Washington, D.C.: US Dept. HEW, 1959.

Wolfensberger, W., and Kurtz, R., eds. *Management of the Family of the Mentally Retarded.* Chicago: Follett, 1969.

Wood, Andrew. *A Manual for Reaching Retarded Children for Christ.* Union Grove, Wisc.: Shepherds, n.d.

Woodward, M. "Early Experience and Behavior Disorders in Severely Subnormal Children." *British Journal of Social and Clinical Psychology* 11 (1963):174-84.